A LIFE in the TREES

This book is dedicated to the memory of my parents, Eddie and Maura, who encouraged an abiding love and appreciation of nature in my siblings and myself.

A LIFE *in the* TREES

A personal account of the
GREAT SPOTTED WOODPECKER

DECLAN MURPHY

With a foreword by
JOHN BOORMAN

Illustrated by
KILLIAN MULLARNEY
and
FLEMMING CHRISTOFFERSEN
With photographs by
DICK COOMBES

THE LILLIPUT PRESS
Dublin

Published by

THE LILLIPUT PRESS LTD

62–63 Sitric Road, Arbour Hill, Dublin 7, Ireland

www.lilliputpress.ie

Text © Declan Murphy, 2019
Photographs © Dick Coombes, 2019
Illustrations © Killian Mullarney, Flemming Christoffersen, 2019

ISBN 978 1 84351 750 4

1 3 5 7 9 10 8 6 4 2

Typeset by Niall McCormack
Printed in Poland by Drukarnia Skleniarz

CONTENTS

FOREWORD

THE WOODPECKER CHOSE a primal wood with no evidence of human activity. Using just its beak it began to drill a deep hole high up in a tree. The familiar knocking sound echoed through the valley. It attracted the attention of a man with the curious eyes of a child.

He searched the wood for the woodpecker, but when the bird heard his approach it would stop drilling until the man left. But the man persisted and eventually identified the nascent nest. The bird waited ... but the man did not go away.

He did not act like a predator; but what did he want? He did not look like a pine marten that could climb the tree and drag the chicks out of the nest!

The man seemed kindly disposed. He kept still.

Well, the nest had to be drilled, so the woodpecker started pecking and knocking again ... with the man watching.

He watched the completion of the nest.

He watched the laying of eggs.

He watched and watched ... until he became part of the wood.

And he relates the fascinating outcome of the story in these pages.

That man is my neighbour, Declan Murphy.

JOHN BOORMAN
July 2017

AUTHOR'S PREFACE

FIRST AND FOREMOST, I am not a scientist, nor do I claim to be an ornithologist. Rather, I am an observer of birds and nature, someone with an insatiable curiosity as to how birds go about their daily business and the environment in which they live.

Watching wildlife remotely using automated cameras or studying from the comfort of a centrally-heated office removes the observer from the true environment of the bird. I have always believed that one can only truly understand a bird's environment by sharing it with the bird and participating in all the ups and downs that it must endure.

Most of the observations listed in the coming pages are my own, and the conclusions and speculations drawn from them are likewise my own. Nature cannot always be identified, categorised and placed in a box as neatly as we may like to think no matter how much we may believe we know about this wonderful world around us, there is always room to wonder.

Throughout my writing of this book I have always felt I was simply the storyteller and that the real credit lay with the large team of supporters who assisted me throughout the book's production. Without them, the story would have remained forever in my head with no stage to play across, and I would like to take this opportunity to introduce you to them.

I am indebted to Pat Casey of Glendalough, the National Parks and Wildlife Service of the Department of Arts, Heritage, Regional, Rural and Gaeltacht Affairs, BirdWatch Ireland and the Heritage Department of Wicklow County Council for their financial contributions and the administrative support they provided; between them they made it happen.

I could not have followed the daily antics of the woodpeckers you will meet in the coming chapters without the support of Kathy Gilfillan and Paul McGuinness, who kindly granted me unlimited access across their property at all hours of the day and night. Their Groundsman, Kevin Singleton, has been stalwart in his support and assistance to me over the past years, and for this I am extremely grateful.

John Boorman provided some wonderful insights and comments on the early drafts of this book. His film, *The Emerald Forest*, provided me with much inspiration for my own quest, and I am delighted that he was prepared to write such a beautiful and evocative foreword to this book.

It has often been said that 'a picture paints a thousand words', in which case the illustrators of this book saved me writing twenty thousand words, or about sixty pages! I consider myself fortunate to have had my work brought to life by not one but two incredibly talented and respected artists. I am honoured and privileged that such an illustrious and world-famous bird artist as Killian Mullarney was prepared to provide the full-page illustration seen in this work. Killian has successfully reproduced the image in my head with a delicacy and vibrancy that leaves me lost in both wonder and admiration. My gratitude cannot be expressed deeply enough, and to Killian I can only say thank you. Flemming Christoffersen provided the illustrations which accompany the chapter headings. His unique style truly captures the essence of the moment and his work brings so much of the story to life, for which I am truly grateful.

The photographs in this book were provided by Dick Coombes, one of the few people in Ireland licensed to photograph great spotted woodpeckers at the nest. With decades of experience in photography, his understanding of the nuances of light are those of a true master, and the pictures he provided for this book are, in my opinion, quite possibly the best ever taken of this species in Ireland. As a trusted mentor, friend and fellow woodpecker enthusiast, Dick provided many invaluable comments during the writing of this book. Furthermore, he provided much additional woodpecker data from other nest sites in Ireland.

Throughout my writing I have frequently, and literally, been lost for words, phrases and even ideas. Early manuscripts had to be rewritten and reworked numerous times due to the diligence of the 'Grammar Police' who nursed me through the convoluted trails of style and helped with my understanding of structure and punctuation. Seamus Bridgeman, Catherine Donnelly, Gerry Donnelly, Angela Mason, Brendan Murray, Declan O'Sullivan and Sheila Townsend all contributed to this mammoth task.

In particular, a special debt of thanks is owed to Niall Hatch, who assisted in so many aspects of the book's production and who endured the thankless, almost endless job of proofreading for months on end.

Finally, I wish to thank my wife Karen and our children, Luke and Emily, who endured my frequent and often lengthy absences with patience and understanding.

Without all of these people and the assistance they provided, the story ahead of you would have remained untold.

INTRODUCTION

HOPE IS A WORD that dominates the mind of a birdwatcher and I have been watching birds since I was seven – or possibly younger – the truth is I can't recall a time that I wasn't infatuated with the natural world around me and the birds, animals and plants that live in it. I grew up in the suburbs of Dublin, and while my parents certainly appreciated the outdoors, they were not, in any manner of speaking, birdwatchers. However they recognised my interest, strange as it may have seemed to them at the time, and did what they could to encourage it by taking me for walks every weekend to the local woods, estuaries, mountains, lakes and the seashore. I had no interest in sport of any sort and even less interest in people, with the exceptions of David Attenborough, Gerald Durrell, Éamon de Buitléar and Gerrit Van Gelderen, all of whom graced my life through their writing and childlike wonder at the world around us. Even as a young boy, I always felt more at ease in the company of nature than that of people, and while this may have seemed unorthodox, or even odd to my parents, they never did anything to deter me from my passion. Quite the opposite, in fact; Christmases and birthdays were marked by a rapidly expanding library of books covering every aspect of nature as I tried to fill my childhood brain with facts and figures about the natural world. I collected all the feathers I found, I kept fragments of eggshells in matchboxes lined with cotton wool and I stored old disused nests, found while searching hedgerows during the winter months, in Clarks shoeboxes under the bed.

Sadly, outside of my family, there was no one to share my interest with. At the time I was growing up, modern environmentalism had not yet emerged and supporting Greenpeace was more likely to have you labelled as an eccentric tree-hugger than raise one's social standing. Quite simply, birdwatchers were a rarity.

The only birdwatching organization in the country during this time was the Irish Wildbird Conservancy, nowadays known as BirdWatch Ireland. Primarily run by volunteers, it had only a small number of branches nationwide which organised events for like-minded people. The Dublin branch was based in the city centre, quite a distance away, and was as unreachable to me then as the planet Mars is to me now. Fortunately, as I entered my early teens, this began to change. A gradual interest in the world around us was beginning to grow and as a result a new branch of the Irish Wildbird Conservancy was founded in the south Dublin area where I lived. Once again it fell to my parents and subsequently my older brothers to facilitate and develop my interest by transporting me to and from the various events held each month; and how that interest developed.

Every month brought two vital dates to my teenage diary. The first Tuesday of the month meant an indoor meeting in a local hotel, where an invited speaker would give a presentation on his or her chosen topic, which could be anything from the science of barnacle geese to the depletion of the ozone layer. To be honest, many of these presentations were not that interesting or relevant to me at that age;

no reflection on the speaker, but more on the fact that very few people of my age attended and as such the speakers were more accustomed to pitching their presentations at an adult audience. However, the first Sunday of each month was a lot more interesting. This was the monthly 'outing', and it was what I lived for, ticking off the days one by one on my calendar.

Each month throughout the year, the branch would meet at a different location to go and look at the birds that could be found there. Led by experienced birdwatchers, with telescopes far more powerful than the 8x30 magnification binoculars I had been given for my birthday, these outings introduced me to birds that until then I had only ever seen in my bird books. Weird-looking birds with wonderful sounding names like 'red-breasted merganser' were no longer confined to page eighteen of my bird book; they now sailed free in my mind as they surged through the waves of Dublin Bay while we watched them from Dun Laoghaire's West Pier. With their spiky punk-rocker hairstyle, these unusual sea ducks are not commonly seen unless you know where to look for them. Looking through telescopes, they could be glimpsed on the sea, bouncing up and down like a bunch of multi-coloured corks, and they weren't alone. Other birds previously only known from books surfaced alongside them: great northern divers, common scoters and long-tailed ducks. For so long these had been static, trapped on the pages of my bird book, but now they had life breathed into them and were finally set free.

When I saw my first red-breasted mergansers, the World Wide Web had not yet been invented, nor had digital photography. The problems I faced watching birds then are barely conceivable now. Nowadays you can use the internet to find out exactly where certain birds live and what they look like before venturing out to look for them. In many cases, you can even see pictures of the exact individual you are hoping to locate before leaving your house; in short, you can appear to be an expert without even seeing the bird. I, on the other hand, had to make do with what now seem like remarkably limited resources. There were only a handful of bird books available that showed anything other than the most common species you were likely to encounter in your garden. The few field guides available that did show a more complete range of birds found throughout Ireland often had poor or inadequate illustrations and lacked details of where to go and look for them. For example, our friend the red-breasted merganser is described as 'widespread in Ireland', but unless you know to look offshore on the open sea then you have little chance of seeing one.

Looking through the growing number of bird books on my bookshelves in the evenings became a daily routine, one I still indulge in many years later. It always seemed so unfair that Ireland had so many fewer types of birds compared to Great Britain, and even more so when compared to Europe. As I poured over the pages while I lay on my bed, it seemed that all the truly spectacular birds and the most brightly coloured species didn't live in Ireland. Where were the eagles? My imagination was fired with images of bleak, windswept Scottish moors being patrolled by golden eagles, their burnished shoulders reflecting the low winter sun as they scoured the snowfields around them for prey. Where were the brightly coloured Bee-eaters, the graceful yet outlandish Avocets with their upturned bills and, most concerning of all, where were the woodpeckers?

Try as I might, I could not get past this stumbling block in my mind. Every one of my bird books had pictures of woodpeckers in them: there were four types breeding in Great Britain alone and eleven on mainland Europe, yet in Ireland – not one. Naturally, being an ambitious teenage birdwatcher, I wanted to see every bird, but none more than woodpeckers – they were weird and colourful. They didn't perch like other birds; they lived in the vertical plane, moving up a tree in the manner of a giant coconut crab. While many other birds nested in holes in trees, none excavated their own holes, digging their way into the timber using nothing other than their bills. This feat of carpentry alone made them stand out above any other species I had seen. Anyone who has tried to sharpen a hardwood stick using a penknife knows how much pressure is required to push the blade into the unyielding wood and yet this bird, using nothing other than its neck muscles and bill, could excavate a cavity deep inside a tree; a feat I could not even attempt...

Was it any wonder that this bird fired my imagination from a young age?

I.
INITIAL ENCOUNTERS

IT WAS MID-NOVEMBER 2007 and I was surveying oak woodland in County Wicklow as part of the Bird Atlas 2007-11, a project co-ordinated by BirdWatch Ireland, the British Trust for Ornithology and the Scottish Ornithologists Club. The survey would cover both the winter and summer season and this was my first atlas visit to this particular wood.

As is often the case during November in the Wicklow Mountains, the air was bitingly clear and crisp and the sky was a pure, peaceful blue that extended, unbroken by cloud, from one horizon to the other. The towering oak trees around me were almost completely bare, the final few remaining leaves clinging stubbornly to the topmost branches despite the late October gales that that had rampaged across the hills for days without end. The ground was thick with their fallen comrades, and as I crunched through the layers of auburn and russet,

I remembered, how when I was ten, I used to imagine they were like cornflakes; back then, to me they looked and sounded just the same as I ran through them, kicking them up in flurries of rustling gold.

This particular oakwood, in a sheltered river valley, differed from other surrounding woodlands in that the trees were well-spaced and far more majestic in both height and girth than the more twisted specimens typically seen alongside the various glaciated lakes and steep valley sides of the Wicklow Mountains. This was more of a parkland setting, an effect enhanced by the lack of a dense ground-layer of vegetation. The bare grey boughs of the oaks against that peaceful blue, coupled with the palette of yellow and orange below, gave me an amazing feeling of wellbeing as I recorded the birds around me that morning. chaffinches were calling *pink* as they rustled through the leaves on the ground, foraging with great tits, blue tits and robins. Counting them was often challenging as they were continuously in motion, flying up to the treetops and then just barely alighting before flying back down again and disappearing into the leaf-filled furrows that wound through the woodland. Woodpigeons and stock doves clamoured noisily on the topmost branches while a single raven gave its gruff, croaking call as it flew high overhead.

The real challenge for a birdwatcher carrying out recording work such as this is not locating the regular, easy-to-find birds, but rather the more secretive, furtive species, which can often only be located and identified by their calls. A Treecreeper gave its high pitched *seeeeep* from a nearby tree, but it was still several minutes before I was able to locate the small silhouette on the underside of a branch as it scuttled along, probing amongst the crevices in the bark for food.

Although widespread in Ireland and occurring wherever there is well-wooded habitat, the treecreeper is a bird with which many people are unfamiliar with. Its small build and mouse-like habits as it runs up the trunk of a tree, coupled with its inconspicuous mottled brown plumage, generally means it goes unnoticed. Many birdwatchers, although familiar with the bird, find the high-pitched song and calls it makes very hard to pick out against the backdrop of other birds' sounds.

While I was watching the treecreeper, a sudden outburst of screeching and raucous calls erupted from a nearby grove of oaks as a family party of jays unexpectedly spotted me. Often called the 'sentinel of the woods', the jay is always on the alert for predators, and its loud calls are a warning both to its comrades and to other birds that trouble is afoot. One of our most colourful birds, and somewhat incongruously a member of the usually drab crow family, the jay is bedecked with shades of pinkish brown, black and white, with an astonishing blaze of electric blue on its wings.

Despite this garish palette, the jay is notoriously difficult to see well. Preferring to remain hidden in the treetops, its harsh cry and a glimpse of its white rump as it flaps weakly from tree to tree are usually all that give away the bird's identity. There were at least five jays in this group: most likely a pair with its offspring, since family groups often remain together until the spring.

I was completely absorbed in these colourful crows going about their business when a loud *KIK* from the surrounding woodland filtered through into my thoughts. My mind half-registered it as 'something different', but pushed it aside as two of the jays began to fight, screeching and flapping like a pair of fighting cocks as they thrashed around in the branches. Any earlier concerns they had about my presence were now long forgotten.

Another *KIK* sounded in the distance, and this time, rather than simply registering at the back of my mind as 'something interesting', it crashed into the forefront of my consciousness with the force of a sledgehammer. 'Great spotted woodpecker' I blurted out loud to no one in particular, as I scrambled to my feet looking frantically in every direction but the correct one. A third *KIK*, more distantly again, indicated that the bird was by now several hundred metres away. I then realised by the loudness of the first call, which had barely registered due to being drowned out by the jays' squabbling, that the bird had been very close, possibly even in the nearest trees. I was furious at myself: I hadn't been quick enough to recognise the call for what it was – but then it was so unexpected.

At this time, great spotted woodpeckers were extremely rare birds and had not yet bred in the Republic of Ireland. To be precise, they were classified as a vagrant, not even a native species. I had only ever seen two before in Ireland, a young bird in Ashford, County Wicklow a couple of years earlier and a female in Annamoe, also in County Wicklow, late the previous December. All thoughts of the survey and counting jays were now gone from my mind, to be replaced by something resembling blind panic as I hurtled through the woodland in the vague direction of where the bird had last called from, clearing bilberry bushes in a single stride and bounding down an escarpment while my mind raced with questions: What age was it? What sex was it? Was it alone? How long had it been here?

All these questions, yet no sign of the bird. I leant against the bole of a large beech trying to catch my breath, when from almost overhead came a loud piercing *KIK...KIK*. I looked up, and there on the trunk of a tree, with his back to me and his head turned around to watch me, was a male great spotted woodpecker.

I watched him for no more than a few seconds before he flew to another tree; however the image of that woodpecker will forever be etched in my mind. Poised in a typical woodpecker stance, his body was sharply inclined to the trunk of the tree, his whole weight resting on the stiff, rigid feathers of his tail, which were slightly spread out, rather like a fan, to provide even more support, while his claws gripped the surface of the tree, firmly anchoring him against gravity. Other birds which perch in trees have three toes pointing forward and a fourth pointing back. However a woodpecker's foot has two toes pointing forward and two pointing backward, in order to provide greater stability when clinging upright on the side of the tree. His long chisel-like bill was pointed skyward while he kept his piercing eye on my movements below.

His plumage was as striking and distinctive as his poise. The soft black of his back was dominated by two broad white shoulder patches, while his wings were an attractive chequerboard pattern. His head was a maze of black stripes on a white background, finished off with a small patch of the deepest crimson on the back of his otherwise black crown. It was this feature that allowed me to identify my woodpecker as a male, since the female has a completely black crown.

He called briefly and then took off, flying up and out of the canopy only to be lost against the blue sky. I was delighted that it was an adult bird, and especially a male, as this raised the prospect that if he remained in the area until the spring he may start drumming[1] and attract a mate. After all, I had seen a female only a mile away almost a year previously so there was reason to be hopeful.

I stayed in the woodland for the rest of that afternoon, completing the survey work I had started and then searching the trees one by one for signs of recent woodpecker activity. For many people, simply seeing the bird is enough, whereas for me I enjoy watching them as they go about their daily lives and how they interact with the world round them. Sharing the world with them opens a door into a hidden landscape of which so many people have little or no awareness. To enter into the world of the woodpecker, or any other creature, you have to learn to see it and to understand it as they do. They don't simply feed or nest in any tree that takes their fancy; to them, each tree in a woodland is an individual. You need to learn to see the trees through their eyes if you hope to follow them or to enjoy more than the fleeting glimpse I had just experienced by a chance encounter. As trees age, pieces of the outer bark start to loosen and peel like flaking, sunburnt skin they fall off exposing bright, fresh wood underneath. Woodpeckers, when feeding, often tear off pieces of bark to get at insects sheltering underneath. Through trial, error and simple observation it is possible to learn the difference between the two procedures and subsequently to know whether a woodpecker has been feeding in a particular area, even if the actual bird remains unseen. Large oak trees in the prime of their lives often dominate the woods in Wicklow, yet during the winter months these offer little attraction to woodpeckers, since the

---

[1] Drumming: The sound a woodpecker makes by rapidly striking its bill against the branch of a tree. It is used to proclaim ownership of a territory.

wood has not yet begun to decay and provide a food source for the beetle grubs upon which woodpeckers often feed. However, during the summer months when the oak trees are in full leaf, woodpeckers will happily forage in them for insects, which they then feed to their young. Examining the trees in a woodland one-by-one takes time, but by mentally crossing off those that are less attractive and locating the key ones it becomes possible to build up a picture of how long woodpeckers have been in an area.

As I searched the woodland that November afternoon I found few signs of activity until I came towards the middle of the woodland. One of the largest oak trees near the centre of the woods was a true 'King of the Forest' and sported a majestic 'stag-head' on its crown. This feature, only found on the oldest of the trees, is formed when the old uppermost branches die off, allowing light into the lower branches and stimulating dormant buds to burst into growth, forming a new, smaller and lower crown. The branches that formed the original high crown were now bare and bleached and their sinuous shapes extended above the lower crown, like the tines of the deer that give the feature its name.

Looking along the branches, backlit against the afternoon sky, my eyes picked out a long row of small holes, each about 2cm across, extending down the length of the branch; it was as though the branch had been strafed by gunfire during a shootout. I had seen these types of markings before in other countries and knew that they were the feeding marks of a woodpecker. Many different beetle larvae feed on decaying wood and their burrows extend throughout the decaying timber. The foraging great spotted woodpecker works his way along the length of the tunnel, boring into it every few centimetres to extract a grub. As he follows the internal wanderings of the larvae he gradually produces a line of 'pits' along the branch, and it was this feature that told me that the individual I had just seen had been here for a while. These feeding pits were never created in a single feeding session but accumulated over a period of time by a woodpecker returning to a favoured feeding spot. Each visit might result in only one or two pits being excavated.

The sight of a long line of them was a fair indicator that a woodpecker had been here for a while. An adult woodpecker would need more than just a single branch full of larvae to sustain him, however, and I continued to search the woodland for the remainder of that afternoon.

Disappointingly, there were relatively few signs that a woodpecker had been residing here for any length of time. Another stag-headed oak, a smaller, less regally imposing individual, showed signs of 'gunfire' across its boughs, while several other trees sported shiny new sapwood, glowing brightly in the late afternoon winter sun, where a feeding woodpecker had removed the surface bark. I couldn't find any winter roosting holes or any indication of a nesting hole from the previous season, so it seemed that this individual had to be quite a recent arrival.

I revisited the area on several occasions during the weeks approaching the winter solstice, but the shortening days combined with the arrival of more typical harsh weather produced no further sightings. Like the hedgehog, which slumbers through the coldest months of the year, I would have to wait until spring.

The following year, spring arrived early for the Wicklow Mountains, temporarily as it turned out. Although February is sometimes regarded in Ireland as the first month of spring, here in the valleys and uplands it is usually cold, bleak and wet. However, an unseasonable anticyclone had settled over Ireland and calm winds and clear skies became the daily pattern for a week or so. I made my way to a clearing near the centre of the wood early one morning, shortly after sunrise. The tops of the trees were lit by the low morning sun and radiated colour against a pastel blue sky dotted with cumulus clouds, while the woodland below remained in shadow; the soil underfoot was still cold, wet and unwelcoming from the past winter's incessant rain. It was quiet as I walked along the rutted, leaf-soaked tracks, with only a nearby song thrush breaking the silence with its classical melodic fluting song, later joined by the distant cawing of rooks from their nests at the edge of the woodland. I was absorbing the tranquillity, which comes from being alone in such a place, when a loud *KIK* erupted nearby.

He was perched on an oak tree about 50m from me and was happily engrossed in extracting a fat white grub with a shiny mahogany head from a rotting limb near the top of the tree. Having succeeded, he quickly swallowed his prize and flew off, bounding through the naked treetops in the same manner as penguins leap through the waters of Antarctica. Moments later, from deep inside the woodland, came a sound so eloquent and beautiful yet so alien to this country that it seemed to belong to another woodland realm; the sound of a woodpecker drumming – and it was the first time I had ever heard it in Ireland.

For me it was this sound, perhaps more than any other, which separated the nature of Great Britain and Ireland. Many British natural history television programmes, atmospheric sound recordings and birdsong recordings all feature the drumming noise that a great spotted woodpecker makes in the spring. A beautiful sound, like a mellow drum-roll on a wooden percussion box, it reverberates throughout the early spring air and into the countryside beyond; yet until now Ireland had been bereft of this acoustic wonder...

It seemed that was now set to change.

PROFILE OF A CARPENTER

THE GREAT SPOTTED woodpecker is about the same size as a blackbird, sporting a striking black and white plumage with a vivid red patch under the tail. The black of its feathers is a true black, unlike those of many other species such as the magpie, which although they may appear black and white are actually washed with iridescent indigo, green and bronze. The red under the tail is typically a deep crimson, although with birds in their first breeding season it is often less vivid. The only visible difference between the sexes is that the male has a small crimson patch on the rear of his head, a feature absent in the female. Young birds usually show a variable amount of red on the forehead and crown which is then lost through moult by early winter. They also have a pale pastel pink wash under the tail. Great spotted woodpeckers have a very characteristic bounding flight that, with experience, can be used to identify it at considerable distance. During their flight, they close their wings on each 'bound', creating a very stumpy appearance when seen flying overhead. They spend most of their time clinging to tree trunks and branches, feeding quietly. Often their distinctive loud *KIK* call is the first indication of their presence. They take their name from the white spots on their wings and from the fact that they are the larger of the two pied woodpeckers found in Great Britain. The other species, the lesser spotted woodpecker is considerably smaller and has never been recorded in Ireland.

Globally, the great spotted woodpecker is a widely distributed species. It occurs in the Canary Islands and North Africa, throughout Europe, across Russia and much of China and as far east as Japan and Kamchatka. There are a number of regional forms across its range, known as subspecies, which can be identified by slight differences in the plumage and body structure. Strangely, until very recently, it was absent from Ireland and only occurred as an occasional vagrant from other countries, usually during the winter.

It has often been a bone of contention amongst scientists and birdwatchers as to whether or not the great spotted woodpecker was resident in Ireland in times past. The argument centres on the prehistoric bones of a great spotted woodpecker found in a cave in Co. Clare. Do the bones represent a viable population or are they merely the sad remains of an isolated, lost individual, like so many other vagrant species which reach our shores each year from other lands, having become lost or disorientated during migration? The importance of this argument revolves around whether the species is expanding and colonizing new territory or recolonizing and returning to former parts of its range, but has little to do with the bird's natural history as a whole.

Aside from this, we had no new information until birdwatchers started recording great spotted woodpeckers as vagrants in the 1800s[2]. The species was never a regular visitor and throughout the twentieth century, decades would pass with no sightings. Those that

---

[2] The Birds of Ireland by Richard Ussher and Robert Warren.

did occasionally show up were invariably found during winter months and most likely were from the Scandinavian population, which is migratory by nature. Most sightings over the years were of single birds.

All that changed in the early 2000s, when the species, for unknown reasons, started to expand its range and birds began arriving on our shores. They were recorded on two offshore islands off the southern coast of Ireland, Great Saltee and Cape Clear, providing clear evidence that the species was arriving naturally. The arrival of birds on the south coast lent weight to the argument that the birds had originated from continental Europe rather than Great Britain.

Following the arrival of these early pioneers, a small breeding nucleus became established in Wicklow and this was felt by birdwatchers such as myself to be of British origin not simply on account of the short distance across the Irish Sea, but also because the population there was expanding. In 2010 a blood sample was taken from an adult female, caught under licence from the National Parks and Wildlife Service, and following analysis of its DNA and also of feathers found in nests in Wicklow, it was conclusively revealed that the Irish population of great spotted woodpeckers had originated in various parts of Great Britain.

Although the breeding population in County Wicklow had originated in Great Britain, the same might not have applied to the individuals seen on the offshore islands along the south coast. Simply by trajectory, it would have been more likely to expect that these originated from Europe, in which case the expansion of this species' range seems to have occurred across a broad front rather than a single point of origin. The expansion of the species range into Ireland coincided with a huge increase in the population across much of its range. In Great Britain there was a four hundred percent increase during the past forty years alone[3] and this increase was mirrored across much of Europe.

---

[3] Bird Atlas 2007–11: The Breeding and Wintering Birds of Britain and Ireland by D. E. Balmer, S. Gillings, B. J. Caffrey, R. L. Swann, I. S. Downie, and R. J. Fuller.

Why a species of woodpecker should suddenly expand its range in this manner is not known for certain, nor is this an event that is confined to woodpeckers. One of the most impressive and unexpected range expansions involved the collared dove. Widely distributed across Ireland and a familiar sight in towns and suburban gardens, the delicately proportioned collared dove only arrived here in 1959. A native of Asia and the Balkan Peninsula, it was a sedentary species and rarely moved more than a few kilometres from where it hatched. For unknown reasons, during the 1930s it suddenly developed a sense of wanderlust and rapidly spread across all of Europe. The first birds were seen in Down, Dublin and Galway[4], and within a decade its monotonous cooing and ubiquitous calls were a familiar sound in Irish towns. Whether or not the great spotted woodpecker will prove to be as successful remains to be seen.

Although great spotted woodpeckers can now be observed throughout the year in Wicklow, the breeding season between February and June provides the best opportunities for prolonged viewing. The process of raising a family seems to occupy their lives far longer than most other birds found in the same habitat, and much of this is due to the effort and commitment involved in excavating the nesting chamber in which they plan to raise their young.

Birds such as the robin and the blackbird can complete their nests in as little as two or three days, whereas the great spotted woodpecker can take up to three weeks to carve its way into the heart of its chosen tree. As I searched for nest holes, I regularly came across what I thought were the beginnings of new ones being excavated. In all cases, a small oval pit had been sunk into the bark to a depth of about 5cm. As the days passed, however, there would be no progression and even when the breeding season had finished they would remain untouched. In the past, they were considered to be 'trial holes', with the assumption being that the birds initially selected the site as suitable, but as excavation proceeded they discovered that the wood was too hard or perhaps too

---

[4] Birds in Ireland by Clive D. Hutchinson.

soft to provide a stable chamber inside. But I have seen these holes both in sound trees and in those already beginning to rot, as well as in trunks in various stages between, so the soundness of the timber appears not to be the issue. It is generally now believed that these unfinished pits are part of a bonding process between the pair and have nothing to do with actual nest construction: the first steps in building and strengthening the union between the pair. Most of these miniature nest holes are constructed early in the season and when the nesting instinct becomes so powerful that proper excavation of a nest hole begins, their creation usually ceases.

While many nest holes are reused by a pair of woodpeckers for several consecutive years, some pairs prefer to excavate a new nest hole each year. Having selected a suitable site, excavation usually starts in early April. Both sexes share the work and will spend several hours each day on the job; however, as with all aspects of the nesting process, it is the male that is most active both when it comes to site selection and excavation.

The initial bore into the trunk is made by the bird striking the wood alternately from the right and then from the left. This produces a wedge-shaped cut that deepens horizontally as the bird tunnels into the wood. The technique of striking the wood is radically different from that used when drumming. When drumming, the bird brings its head back and rapidly strikes the wood with its bill held close to the timber. The extreme force required for each rapid burst is generated by the neck muscles. During excavation the bird uses not only these powerful muscles but also those of its shoulders and back. Clinging to the tree and bracing himself using his reinforced tail feathers, he swings his head and strikes the wood with his bill, in the same manner as a forester swings a felling axe to split a log. Several alternating swings are required to produce a chip of wood less than a quarter the size of your little finger nail.

One day, as an experiment, I tried to reproduce the woodpecker's efforts using a knife on a fallen tree trunk. After a few initial tiny flakes had been cut away, I failed to make any further headway. Try as I might, I could not chip out anything resembling even a small pit by using the swinging technique of a woodpecker. Only by leaving the blade in the wood and pressing my full weight on it was I able to bore a small hole. The woodpecker's bill is half the width of the blade on my Swiss Army knife, yet it successfully carves its way into the tree. I have nothing but admiration for this little carpenter.

Having created a wedge-shaped opening, the woodpecker then proceeds to work around the edges to make an elliptical shaped entrance. Every few minutes, the bird stops its tunnelling and throws the accumulated wood chips out of the hole with a sideways flick of the head. The ground below the entrance hole gradually becomes littered with them, their bright colour contrasting with the dark green moss upon which they come to rest. This first stage of building the nest chamber is carried out in less than a week, but then the work gets harder, and as a result, becomes slower. Tunnelling in as far as it can reach by swinging its head while clinging to the outside of the tree, it now changes direction and starts excavating downwards. To do so, it must squeeze inside the entrance hole, which restricts how far it can swing its head back to hammer at the wood. As a result, it takes far longer to carve each wood chip. To further complicate matters, the birds now have to stop tunnelling and turn around to throw the wood chips out of the hole before turning back to carry on. It can take a further two weeks to excavate the nest chamber fully, during which time the pair will never be too far from each other, for nest building strengthens the bond between them.

This feat of tunnelling into wood certainly sets woodpeckers apart from any other bird species in Ireland. And, as if that wasn't enough, the sounds they create and the ways in which they create them distinguish them even further. Birds are classified into groups known as orders. Most of our common garden birds belong to the order known as the Passerines, often referred to as 'songbirds', however, woodpeckers belong to a different order known as Piciformes. Woodpeckers and their fellow members of this order share characteristics such as a long barbed tongue, reinforced skull and stiffened tail feathers — features not found on other birds encountered in Irish gardens. Although woodpeckers may be more closely related to many familiar garden birds than they are to, say ducks or gulls, they have no operatic tendencies or skills.

Strangely, great spotted woodpeckers are one of the few birds encountered in gardens and woodland that actually cannot sing, in the sense that they do not have specific territorial vocalisations. Even familiar birds not generally thought of as songbirds, such as magpies, swallows, jays and starlings have astonishingly beautiful songs once you learn to recognise them. Yet, despite not being able to sing, woodpeckers are renowned for the distinctive sounds they make to proclaim their territory and to attract a mate.

There is no sound that, to my ears at least, is more evocative of woodland in early spring than that of a great spotted woodpecker drumming. This term is used to describe the act of a woodpecker rapidly striking a resonant piece of wood with its bill, creating a sound reminiscent of a drum roll. Different branches and trees produce different sounds due to the nature of the wood itself, in particular due to its size and whether or not it is deadwood or sapwood. As recently as the early twentieth century, it was not known how woodpeckers actually produced this sound and there were several conflicting arguments. It was considered by some that the sound could not be produced by a bird striking the wood directly with its bill at high speed as the force of the impact would surely kill the bird. Others suggested that the bird used the wood as a form of amplifier, placing its bill into a small hole and making a sound using its tongue, rather like a person 'clicking' theirs. Only when birds were filmed and the footage was played back in slow motion could it be ascertained beyond all doubt that the sound was produced by the physical act of the bird striking the wood with its bill. Close-up filming of great spotted woodpeckers drumming, carried out in Germany in the late 1950s, showed that woodpeckers would strike the tree up to fourteen times per second.

Watching the male perform his drumming over the course of the spring made me realise that it had to be more than a simple proclamation of 'Keep out, this is my territory' being broadcast across the cold early spring landscape. Sometimes the burst of drumming was loud, strident and clearly audible for almost a kilometre on a clear day. Its precise, evenly spaced tattoo was the enigmatic sound that so many people associate with the woodpecker. Invariably the performance would take place on a small branch, most likely hollow and seemingly chosen to provide maximum resonance. But then the male would change to a slightly different branch, sometimes only a couple of metres away, and it was as though the volume of a radio had been turned from ten down to about three.

The drumming produced in such circumstances might only be audible at a range of one hundred metres and is therefore unlikely to contribute in any manner to territorial proclamation. This type of drumming seemed to be produced on branches that were fully alive and therefore had far less resonance than deadwood. I have seen both male and female woodpeckers performing a duet on the same tree using this quiet drumming and it is possible that it is a pair-bonding exercise. Although I have sometimes seen the male performing this quiet drumming alone with no indication of a female in the immediate vicinity, their habit of sitting quietly in the canopy means it is almost impossible to confirm whether the female is truly absent.

As well as drumming, great spotted woodpeckers make a number of distinctive and readily identifiable calls. They call for a variety of reasons: to keep in contact with a mate, to warn chicks in the nest of a predator or to warn off an intruder. In the same way that drumming can be frequently heard one day and not the next, the same applies to their calls. Some days they can be extremely vocal, calling throughout the day, whereas on other days the birds can be completely silent for hours on end.

The most regularly heard call is the loud, strident *KIK* which is often repeated at five second intervals. When hearing this upon entering a wood, it usually means 'You've been spotted' and the woodpecker will usually call several more times before flying off. They often give this call as they fly and in many cases when I am searching the woods for woodpeckers outside the breeding season, this call combined with a glimpse of a bird disappearing into the canopy is the only indication that they are present at all.

This single note call can be uttered in a variety of ways depending on the circumstances. A bird that has been disturbed or has unexpectedly spotted a predator will utter it with tremendous force – *KIK* – whereas a relaxed bird calling to its mate nearby will use it more softly – *kik*. A lone bird feeding in the tree canopy can often be heard quietly calling as though to itself *kik... kik... kik... kik... kik*.

Most bird field guides list this *KIK* call as the only sound the great spotted woodpecker makes, aside from the drumming they make in the spring, but this is far from being the case and the repertoire of this species is quite complex.

During the breeding season, a whole new range of sounds uttered by both sexes will fill the canopy. The most frequently heard is a 'rattling' or 'churring' sound similar to that made by the mistle thrush in flight. It is always made by a bonded pair and usually occurs near to their chosen nest site. When checking territories in springtime, it is a useful indicator that a pair is present and that a potential nest site is close by. This sound is also made when the male and female are performing their nuptial flight as they weave their way amongst the tangled canopy branches in a dizzying display of aerial speed and agility. Similar to this rattle is a slightly higher pitched 'whinnying' sound not unlike the breeding calls of the male little grebe found on the nearby lakes. Unlike the rattle, this call seems to be made only by the female and mostly occurs in the weeks prior to the eggs hatching; for example, she can often be heard to utter it when changing places with the male at the nest during incubation.

In the days immediately prior to egg laying, the pair remain close to each other and rarely seem to stray from each other's sight. During this time they regularly call to each other using a very quiet 'cheeping' sound, a sound which always reminds me of those made by the budgerigars I kept as a boy, as they settled down to sleep. It is a content, sleepy-sounding call and I often wondered if it was a form of reassurance or a way of further strengthening the bond between them in the final days before the eggs are laid. As well as the rattles and whinnying sounds I have often heard a loud 'chuckling' sound, usually made by the male and only when he is either arriving or leaving a nest that contains eggs.

Many of these sounds are variations on a theme, and to those unfamiliar with bird sounds they may even sound the same. However, the subtle differences must convey a whole range of meanings between the birds and there is no doubt that often they are engaging in the woodpecker equivalent of a human conversation. Young woodpeckers are equally as noisy as their parents, especially in the final week before they leave the nest and the calls they make from within the tree gradually change as they develop up until they take their first flight, at which point they are almost inseparable from those of their parents.

To find proof that the great spotted woodpecker was breeding in Ireland was my Holy Grail. In an unusual start to my quest, the first proof of breeding did not involve finding a nest with young. Instead, the first evidence came when a young great spotted woodpecker turned up on a peanut feeder in a rural garden on the Dublin/Kildare border in July 2008 – and naturally I went to see it. It was to be a memorable day for me; my first ever sighting of a young woodpecker in Ireland and the first of my encounters with them as an Irish breeding species. I certainly didn't realise then how many more I would see in the coming years.

It was evening when a friend and I arrived at the garden and the sun was still quite high in the sky. Unlike the native, unkempt woodlands of the Wicklow Mountains, where most of the sightings of woodpeckers would be made in the next few years, this garden was manicured in its appearance and conjured up images of a stereotypical English country garden. Graceful sweeping lawns surrounded the house like pristine bowling greens, sharply contrasting with the ordered beauty of the perennial flower borders interspersed with geometrically perfect conifers reminiscent of Exocet missiles on a launching pad. As we made our way along the driveway, which meandered through this perfection like a fat, lowland river it was hard to believe that quite possibly the rarest known breeding bird in Ireland at this time was somewhere in the nearby farmland.

We joined the owners in their house and sat for almost half an hour happily drinking tea and munching biscuits before the bird arrived. 'Arrived' is possibly the wrong phrase, as, without any advance warning, it seemed simply to appear on the upright pole that supported the bird table, from which hung several peanut feeders. It was these peanut feeders which had lured this youngster out of its natural habitat and into this artificially created landscape. It clung to the upright pole in the same manner as it would cling on to a large sprawling oak, its body sharply inclined at a forty-five degree angle as it looked cautiously around before hesitantly hopping up along the pole until it reached the peanut feeders and began to feed. This particular youngster sported a complete crimson crown, a diagnostic feature of young birds shown in every bird identification book; yet in future years I would come to realise that this is one of the most variable of all plumage features and not as diagnostic as many bird books might suggest. After spending several minutes quietly feeding, it suddenly raised its head and called loudly before flying off, bounding across the bowling-green lawns and disappearing into the patchwork of surrounding fields with their broken and disjointed hedgerows.

This youngster had only started visiting the garden in the preceding few days and was never accompanied by an adult, or even a sibling, and after another few days he simply vanished with no indication of whence he had come from nor where he had gone. We explored the surrounding fields and countryside that bordered the garden, anticipating that we would find indications of where the youngster had been reared but it proved a fruitless exercise. The nearby tightly grazed sheep swards, divided by sprawling and dense Blackthorn hedges interwoven with bent and twisted wire fencing, provided few feeding opportunities and no nesting sites for woodpeckers. Although they regularly visit gardens, they are primarily a woodland species, needing mature trees both for feeding and nesting. While large gardens and well-wooded parklands can easily meet their requirements, open farmland is unsuitable and far less attractive. Less than a kilometre away was an area of clear-fell coniferous woodland which at first we thought may have held the answer.

For me, a clear-fell wood is one of the most unattractive habitats to pass through; possibly because it is entirely man-made. Reminiscent of a post-apocalyptic landscape, the twisted, broken and bleached limbs of the slaughtered trees lay tangled and entwined across the ground. Several bare and broken trunks still remained upright, scattered randomly like sentinels across the clear-fell, but they contributed nothing to the environment except for their stark, defined silhouettes. The sustainable harvesting of natural resources does not come without its downside and, for me, the scene in front of us was one such disadvantage. The machines that worked this area were long gone as this was a wood which had been processed several years ago. There was nothing here that would provide any attraction for a great spotted woodpecker, and we were no closer to discovering where he had come from.

I never saw another woodpecker in this area, nor did anyone else that I know of, and this initial sighting of an Irish-bred woodpecker, so powerful in its significance, remains an enigma. As woodpeckers became more established in central Wicklow and slowly expanded their range over the coming years, that garden set amongst the farmland remained far outside their central base of operations, almost like a satellite territory. In hindsight, it would seem that this youngster who appeared in 2008 most likely came from one of the territories which were subsequently discovered in the Wicklow Mountains from 2009 onwards. Although many woodpecker families remain together in the same area after they leave the nest, perhaps the very first successful families, completely cut off from others of their kind by the Irish Sea, simply dispersed across the countryside like true pioneers blazing a new trail.

The sighting of that young woodpecker I watched feeding on the peanut feeder that late July evening came less than five months after I had watched my first woodpecker drumming in Ireland. Although we didn't know it at the time, the encounter with that young woodpecker heralded the arrival of a golden age of woodpecker watching for both myself and my friend. Those early years saw many oakwoods in County Wicklow explored and searched for signs of woodpeckers; most were empty, but gradually a small and slowly increasing population began to make its presence felt as woodland after woodland was discovered to have woodpeckers in it. And, with that expansion of birds, so milestone after milestone was achieved, such as:

The first sighting of great spotted woodpeckers performing their courtship display in Ireland ...

The first sighting of them mating ...

And finally, after hours and weeks of searching, watching, waiting and thinking that it could never happen ... they commenced breeding. To the utter disbelief of the dedicated team of observers, the milestones accelerated like a snowball down a mountainside ...

The first sighting of them together at a nest hole ...

The first sighting of them carrying food to a nest ...

The first glimpses of youngsters peering out at the world from the depths of their home ...

The youngsters' first flight into the new world awaiting them ...
and so on.

Each achievement was seen as a rung on a ladder or as part of a picture, and different observers, working as part of a team, noted the various achievements and claimed the glorious trophies in a variety of habitats across County Wicklow. The low breeding density and thin distribution of the species during those first years often meant that different pairs provided different milestones. The first pair observed mating was not the same pair to be first witnessed at a nest hole feeding youngsters. As the woodpeckers increased their numbers with each passing year, those halcyon days of endless discoveries, achievements and wonders were gradually replaced with long-term, data-based studies. For me and the friends that accompanied me, those early days of exploration and adventure can never be replaced – or forgotten.

Although I knew it was probably too much to hope for, I had lived with the possibility that the male I had encountered while conducting my survey might have attracted a mate and raised a family. Throughout February 2008 he continued to fill the woods with the sound of his drumming; but as spring had slowly begun to move northwards that year and with his declaration unanswered, that woodland of my dreams had fallen silent. I have often wondered how long he had beaten out his tattoo on those stag-headed trees before finally flying off in search of a mate elsewhere. And as he searched the wooded valleys and hills of Wicklow for a mate, so my fellow observers and I searched for signs of him or any other woodpeckers that may have accompanied him on his voyage across the Irish Sea.

Starting from the clearing with the stag-headed oak, we searched nearby, and finding nothing, we then went further afield. We followed rumours of 'strange-looking birds' and 'strange sounds' that different people encountered while dog walking and hiking throughout Wicklow that spring. But Wicklow is a large county and the number of woodpeckers living there at that time was likely still only in single figures, so the search was a long one. Nevertheless, through perseverance and fieldcraft over many weeks and months, combined with some good fortune, we encountered woodpeckers in several woodlands during that spring.

Usually it was the male performing his drumming which came to our attention and many of the sightings I had that year were simply of a bird silhouetted against the grey, early morning sky as he perched, seemingly precariously, on the side of a dead branch at the top of a tree before flying off. The novelty of hearing Irish woodlands resonating with the sound of their drumming easily offset the frequently disappointingly brief sightings we were subjected to, despite long hours of waiting. Sightings of females that year were few, but one observer was fortunate enough to witness a nuptial flight as part of courtship display. In subsequent years, I too have been fortunate enough to see this behaviour on numerous occasions, yet it always fills me with wonder each time I witness it due to its intimacy and uniqueness. During their courtship, the male and female will often face each other, calling excitedly, and sometimes even raising the feathers on their heads before taking off and flying up and out of the canopy. Flying alongside each other, on stiff wings with unusually rapid wing beats, they then complete a frenzied chase in a circuit around their territory, all the time uttering high-pitched trilling sounds as they weave between and twist around the topmost branches of the still leafless oaks. In subsequent years, as I was searching new woodlands, the sight and sound of this high-speed chase through the treetops was always a heart warming moment because it was the sound of love. It was only ever performed by a mated pair on breeding territory.

Yet despite the sighting of a mated pair, and although several other male birds had been heard drumming at other locations during the spring of that year, no nests were located. Until that young woodpecker was seen on the Dublin/Kildare border, there was no indication that breeding had actually taken place. But that sighting combined with the courtship displays earlier in the year merely strengthened our resolve and determination for the quest and the following year, in 2009, not just one but seven nests were finally located in County Wicklow. Of course, it is not known exactly when great spotted woodpeckers first commenced breeding in Wicklow. The first nests were only found in 2009 but woodpeckers had been seen in the same woods in the preceding two years. It is conceivable that they were breeding unrecorded for several years prior to this.

Although widely dispersed across the county and often quite far apart from each other, most seemed to be along the well-wooded valleys of the Avonmore River. This river flows from the glaciated lakes of Lough Tay and Lough Dan, through the valley of Annamoe and on into the Vale of Clara. Many of the valleys carved through these mountains are glacial in origin but the rivers flowing through the moraines, deposits left by the retreating glaciers, have shaped the landscape further, providing a varied and intricate world of rock, bilberry and oak that has proven so attractive to these pioneering birds.

Seven years later, in 2016, thirty-five nests were located in County Wicklow, with a further four nests located in other counties, along with numerous sightings of youngsters. Undoubtedly, there were more than thirty-five pairs of great spotted woodpeckers in County Wicklow, as the number of nests recorded is only a reflection of the effort put in by those endlessly searching tree after tree, woodland after woodland.

It is reasonable to assume that the species will continue to expand its range and in the coming years spread further across the country. The number of pairs in County Wicklow will also quite likely increase and already woodlands that had held only one pair in 2010 held two or three pairs in 2016. The early colonists enjoyed far less competition for territories than many of the current birds and as a result were able to occupy the prime habitat first.

A bird's habitat is nothing other than the landscape in which it chooses to live, feed and rear its young. Some birds are highly adaptable and live in a variety of habitats. Starlings, for example, can be found not only in cities but also in farmland, whereas other species are less adaptable, such as golden eagles, which are usually only encountered in rugged mountainous terrain. In Great Britain, great spotted woodpeckers live in a variety of habitats. They are well accustomed to people there and are frequent visitors to garden bird tables. When the first woodpecker colonists arrived in Ireland they had a wide range of habitat to choose from. Coming from Great Britain to Wicklow, they first encountered the gardens and parklands along the east coast of Ireland and then, farther inland, the wooded lowlands at the foothills of the Wicklow Mountains, yet they seemingly ignored this tame, mellow and managed landscape and struck out for the rugged mountain valleys. There they carved a living in a habitat far more hostile than that which they had traversed. The winter temperatures in the valleys along the Avonmore River have dropped as low as $-14°c$, with even lower temperatures on the exposed escarpments above. Unquestionably, the diversity of life in an oakwood is far richer than that of other Irish woodlands; however, the species is adaptable enough in Great Britain and throughout Europe and Asia to live in parks and gardens. In this context, I found it interesting to see that its initial choice for settlement in Ireland was not the first habitat it passed through but a more challenging landscape that it could hardly have known existed as it advanced farther inland.

Interestingly, although the species is expanding in every direction from Wicklow, it has failed to make any inroads towards Dublin. Wandering individuals have periodically turned up in the various large parks, which grace the suburbs of the city and a bountiful food source in the form of garden peanut feeders is to be found in numerous adjoining gardens, yet they have failed to establish anything other than a tenuous presence. In Great Britain, they also regularly visit gardens for another food source, one which they seem to have so far ignored in this country – blue tits.

The blue tit, one of our most familiar garden birds, regularly nests in the wooden nestboxes that feature in so many of our gardens. However, the great spotted woodpecker has learnt to carve a hole in the side of these nestboxes and take the young blue tits out to feed to its own young. Perhaps when the Irish population of woodpeckers learns of this feeding bonanza they will finally settle into the suburbs of Dublin. Although the parks surrounding the capital are often well-wooded, they rarely include the slow-growing oak tree. Oaks are native to Ireland and most of the woodpeckers in Wicklow favoured them as their nesting tree of choice, occasionally choosing other native species such as ash or birch. The spanish chestnut, however, is not native but originates on the European mainland where it is much prized for both its wood and its fruit. Since the woodpeckers' first arrival, only one pair of had singled out this species of tree for its nest site, marking them out as being different...

But being different is merely another way of being interesting and my interest in woodpeckers was growing.

3 ·
IN THE WOODS

A NUMBER OF YEARS had passed since those initial sightings and it was now 08.30 on a bitter cold morning in mid-February 2015. The woodland that I was making my way towards was located in the sheltered lee of a hill. The sun would need several more hours before it climbed high enough in the sky to cast its strengthening warmth into the depths of this frozen oakwood. This was my third visit in as many weeks and thus far I had failed to find any sign of my quarry.

Just getting to the site was proving challenging enough. The tracks through the woods and alongside the river had either been washed away in the storms or had become so rutted and frozen that driving was impossible. Even travelling by car on the nearby salt-gritted main roads required great care. As I made my way through the frozen countryside, there was little sound, apart from my footsteps splintering the icy puddles and the distant drone of traffic on the road. There was no birdsong, it was too early in the year for that here in the Wicklow uplands. Finches, tits and thrushes gave periodic calls as they went about their daily business of surviving the winter months.

Finally I arrived at my destination, a holly tree overlooking a glade of oak and beech, and settled myself in against the base of the trunk. I pulled the hoodie I was wearing over my tingling ears to try and give them some protection against the frigid air. Taking off my gloves, I plunged my hands into my armpits to try and warm them. I sat waiting; the minutes passed and the cold deepened, driving its icy tendrils deeper into my joints. There was little activity in the woods at this time: a robin hopped along the leaf-littered ground, almost touching my legs, while a treecreeper flew across the track and alighted on the base of an oak tree before beginning its upward spiralling in search of small insects and spiders hiding in the cracks and crevasses of the gnarled bark. These birds seem mouse-like as they scuttle up the trunk; that is, until they reach the top and fly off to the next tree.

I was still admiring the mottled brown plumage of the treecreeper when suddenly I heard a loud burst like the abrupt staccato discharge of a machine gun, and only 30m from where I was sitting. I turned my head and there on the top of a nearby tree stump was my target – a male great spotted woodpecker.

The woodland in which I sat was situated on a steep slope on the eastern side of the Avonmore River, which flowed through a valley in the Wicklow Mountains, extending from Lough Dan, near Roundwood, to Rathdrum. An unsurfaced track, which was rutted but drivable, ran alongside this river for a kilometre before ending at the bottom of a steeply inclined slope. From here an uneven rocky track led upwards through the trees and eventually, after some distance, out onto open moorland. It is deciduous woodland, primarily consisting of oak and beech and a small amount of spanish chestnut, with a variety of individual pines and spruces mixed throughout. The groundcover is sparse with a light covering of bilberry bushes – often referred to as wild blueberries or *Fraughans* in Ireland.

50m up this slope was a small glade, at the centre of which stood a single spanish chestnut tree. It wasn't the only example of this non-native species within the woodland; there were several other larger and more magnificent specimens for this wood had been planted and was not part of a primordial landscape. However, this spanish chestnut was different from the others because a pair of great spotted woodpeckers had nested in it since 2011, although most likely the original birds were not the current tenants. Standing in front of the tree, I found it hard to believe that this was to be my fifth year watching woodpeckers rearing a family in this spot. Memories of watching the youngsters emerging from the nest were so vivid they seemed to be from yesterday rather than four years ago.

The tree was alive, but only just – most of its branches were long gone, torn off by the winter storms that rip through the Wicklow Mountains each winter. Each passing year saw the tree reduced more and more until it was now nothing but a bare trunk with broken spurs along its sides and a few spindly branches here and there sporting a handful of leaves as a meagre contribution to the ancient and diverse ecology of this woodland. Its gnarled, twisted trunk indicated an age older than most humans would live, yet without cutting it down there was no way to be certain. It had certainly stood here for a hundred years, and quite likely more than that. Silhouetted against the sky, its contorted shape almost looked human to my eyes, its upward-reaching boughs like arms raised skyward.

The tree itself, despite being unattractive on account of its lack of canopy or shapely form, caught the eye for several reasons. Firstly, it had an amazing display of extremely large white bracket fungus arranged in a descending cascade, with the largest at the top. Bracket fungus is an indicator that the tree has reached the final stages of its life, and I knew that the unseen centre of the tree would be well-rotted due to the action of this fungus. Secondly, and more importantly as far as I was concerned, the tree was covered both in woodpecker nest holes and feeding holes. Five separate nesting holes had been made in this tree since the birds had first selected it as a nest site five years

In the Woods

ago, and in four of those years they had successfully produced fledged[5] young. The fifth hole had been excavated the previous year, 2014. However, it was not used to rear that year's family and I wondered whether they might select this one to use in the coming season.

The woodpeckers that nested in this tree always carved their own story, paying no heed to the norm to which their forefathers in other countries had adhered to for generations. Most books and studies concerning this species show an average egg-laying date of mid-May, with birds fledging in mid-June. This tree had always seen the young flying well before the end of May, making it amongst the earliest of all woodpecker fledgings in Ireland; earlier, indeed, than the vast majority recorded in Great Britain by the British Trust for Ornithology. The woodpeckers which nested in the spanish chestnut tree also habitually located their nest hole far lower than at any of the other known sites in Wicklow. The first nest hole in this tree was located only two metres above the ground. When the breeding season was over and the nest was no longer being used, it was actually possible to look into the nest hole by standing on a milk crate.

Studies of other nest sites in County Wicklow have shown that woodpeckers seem to favour the north-facing side of a trunk for their nest entrances, yet this tree had nest holes pointing to all four points of the compass. The standard model obviously did not apply to this territory – it was all to play for, and the past few years here have shown that wildcards were part of the daily routine and only the unexpected could be expected. This season was to be no different.

It was a bright sunny morning in early March, and a mistle thrush was hammering out its wild melodic chiming as I stood in the clearing assessing the nest tree. It was still there after the winter storms, and that was a good start – however, of the birds there was no sign, not that I was bothered by this, since woodpeckers are often elusive at the best of times. I only had limited time in which to study the birds this particular year and I was hoping to try to watch them excavating a new

---

[5] Fledged: Fully feathered young that have left the nest.

nest chamber. If they were going to cooperate with me then they should have started by now, but the tree showed no signs of new activity. The previous year's nest holes were all starting to decay around the edges, and I suspected that the inside walls were also beginning to rot. The exception to all this was the new hole, located quite low, which had been excavated sometime during the previous year, oddly after the end of the breeding season. Although great spotted woodpeckers do not mate for life, some pairs do stay together for more than a single season. I couldn't help but wonder whether a pair of woodpeckers might excavate a nest hole months in advance to avoid being under pressure at the start of the following breeding season. Woodpeckers sometimes make roost holes, which are shallower than nest chambers, which they use during the winter months if no suitable nest hole is available for them to sleep in. The male usually remains in the territory throughout the winter to defend it, and often roosts in the previous year's nest hole. However, since there were four other nest holes in the tree, it was hard to believe that this pair had felt the need to excavate another simply so that they would have somewhere to spend the dark winter nights. I was hopeful that they would continue to use this tree during the coming months, provided that there were still woodpeckers in the area. I hadn't seen or heard any, but I was sure it was just a matter of time…an indication of just how much time can be found in the following extracts from my field notes:

2 March (10.30–11.30)
No signs of activity at nest tree, no calls or sightings of birds in the area
4 March (09.30–10.45)
Walked through the woodland and along by the river. Amazing patterns of frost on the frozen leaves on the ground. No sightings or calls.
9 March (15.00–16.30)
Watched the nest tree for over an hour, nothing seen or heard – numb with cold so walked throughout the

*territory for half an hour – nothing, whole area feels
deserted. Beginning to suspect birds may have moved on
this year.*

18 March (10.30–12.30)

*Having been away for well over a week I had high hopes
today, but the absence of birds and calls continues. Have
to widen the search area but hard to know where to
begin. Saw a female goosander[6] on the river as I arrived,
so hopefully she might breed.*

Towards the end of March, I was starting to consider the possibility
that the woodpeckers had decided upon a new location for that year's
nest. I knew from my previous observations of other pairs that a new
nest was usually located within roughly a two hundred metre radius
from the old one. Due to their secretive behaviour, the woodpeckers'
nest could well have remained hidden until the young were old enough
that their hungry begging calls in the nest would have helped me
pinpoint their location. But then my luck changed:

23 March (10.30–12.30)

*Arrived 10.30 and watched the nest tree from a range
of about one hundred metres, all quiet except for a red
squirrel feeding in the trees overhead, scampering along
the most unbelievably thin twigs. Lovely cold, crisp
morning.*

*11.25 – FINALLY – Bird called nearby and the male
landed on the nest tree and began drumming: drummed
three times in quick succession before flying off.*

*11.50 – female simply appeared silently on side of tree.
Sat quietly feeding for about five minutes before flying off
towards the river, no calls heard.*

---

[6] Goosander : A very scarce species of duck in Ireland which breeds in tree holes close
to fast flowing rivers, chiefly in County Wicklow.

These excerpts from my field notes give an indication of the time involved in watching this species and how elusive it can be. I have often met fellow birdwatchers who were fortunate enough to have seen a male in the spring as he drummed on a dead branch, or who watched a bird regularly visiting a peanut feeder. Naturally, this has often led them to form the opinion that the species is very easy to see and straightforward to watch. In my experience, however, they can be incredibly secretive.

I was unable to visit the woods during the rest of the month, but I was now satisfied that the site was still occupied and that the indications were that my woodpeckers would most likely use the new nest hole, since it was by now rather late in the season for them to start excavating.

I was curious, however, as to why they had been so elusive during late February and early March. These months are a time when other territories in the surrounding area usually show a period of intense woodpecker activity, with display flights and drumming duets a regular occurrence, yet this pair had almost slipped under the radar. Although great spotted woodpeckers are today widely distributed in County Wicklow, they occur at a density considerably lower than that in other countries; as a result, competition for breeding territories is minimal. I suspect that the birds know this and do not waste time unnecessarily proclaiming and defending a territory. While they do not pair for life, they do form long-term relationships, which often last longer than just a single breeding season. Because of this, the male may not need to drum each spring to attract a mate; she may have remained on the territory with him during the winter months. Furthermore, if there are no other woodpeckers in the immediate vicinity then there is no need for him to spend time drumming to ward off rivals, simply because none are present. As a result, isolated pairs such as mine can go about their lives with very little evidence of their whereabouts.

I returned to the woods in early April, the first month of the year when spring can truly be said to have arrived in the Wicklow Mountains. All the hopes and aspirations of March had now come to fruition. With the sun climbing higher above the horizon each day, the air was now warmer and the days were longer. The surrounding landscape responded with an outburst of growth and rebirth.

The hedgerows alongside the river were now veiled in a gauze of green as the buds on the hawthorn trees started to swell and burst, and leaves of bluebells were starting to emerge, carpeting the ground with a dark green which would be replaced by a blanket of shimmering blue when the flowers opened during May. As I drove along the riverside track, I watched the ceaseless journeying of blackbirds, dunnocks and song thrushes carrying food to their nests, where broods of fast-growing chicks lay hidden from prying eyes. Parent birds, weighed down with bills full of worms, skimmed across the front of the car, almost touching it as I drove along the track. That time of year always sees a large increase in the number of adult birds, especially blackbirds, killed on our roads by colliding with cars as they dart across.

During those first days of April, I enjoyed several sightings of both the male and the female feeding close to the nest tree. On one occasion I was treated briefly to a duet, with the female drumming in response to the male who was on a different tree only a few metres away. This duetting seemed to have more to do with strengthening the bond between the pair than warding off rivals, as there was never any response from any other woodpecker further afield and the female always responded the moment her mate had finished.

The 10 of April saw an interesting new development. As I arrived, I looked at the nest tree through my binoculars and immediately noticed what appeared to be the beginnings of a new hole about 10cm to the right of the previous year's nest hole – perhaps I was going to be able to watch a nest being excavated after all. I walked closer to get a better look and a bird began calling agitatedly in the trees above me: *KIK... KIK... KIK* followed by a rattling *chhuuuurrr*. This unusual and infrequently heard sound immediately caught my attention, as it is very much a sound one only hears during the breeding season. I knew from previous years' observations that this grating rattle indicated an established territory, and also that the female was close to egg-laying.

Suddenly, and quite unexpectedly, when I was only about 10m from the tree, a bird popped its head out of the previous year's nest hole and eyeballed me. I stood there in amazement and didn't even have a chance to check if it was the male or female before it popped its head back in again. I quickly started to retrace my steps to avoid any disturbance, and as I did so the male landed in the canopy nearby calling *KIK............ KIK............ KIK.* I looked around and saw a head looking out of the nest hole again – I raised my binoculars and confirmed that it was the female before she shot back out of view again.

I moved about one hundred metres back from the spanish chestnut and sat crouched under a low holly bush. Satisfied that I was reasonably well-hidden, I watched the tree for the next thirty minutes, but, alas, there was no activity. My mind was racing – what was going on? The female was behaving as though she was incubating, yet egg-laying should have been weeks away. She was hardly going to sit in the hole for another two or three weeks before even laying an egg, was she?

After that half hour had passed I began to make my way back to my car. As I passed the nest tree, about 30m to my right, the male called loudly overhead and once again the female looked out of the nest hole, staring directly at me, so she was certainly not just 'checking the wallpaper' in the same manner that blue tits often do, flying in and out of the nest box in the weeks before they build their nests – no, this was something different entirely.

Later that night, while reading reports of some of the woodpecker studies carried out in Germany in the 1960s, I found an interesting snippet about black woodpeckers, Europe's largest species of woodpecker and one which breeds as close to Ireland as Brittany. When they finish excavating a new nest hole, seemingly the female will often take up residence in order to prevent other hole-nesting birds, such as stock doves and, in particular, starlings, from commandeering it. This was a different species of woodpecker and the nest hole in question wasn't new, nor were there any starlings in the wood, but the similarities in behaviour were notable.

The nest hole that they spent most of their time investigating, and therefore the one most likely to be used, was located on the north-facing side of the tree. It would therefore be in the shade for most of the day, with the exception of early morning and late evening when it would be lit by low sunlight from the side; a situation that was far from ideal for either observation or photography. By pure chance, there was a pair of trees about twenty-five metres north-east of the nest tree that could conceivably host a temporary hide I might build between them with relatively little effort. However, because the bird was only occupying the nest hole at present and most likely not actually sitting on eggs, I decided not to make any attempt at hide construction in case she changed her mind and moved to an alternative nesting tree. Woodpeckers, as with many other birds, sit tightly on their eggs once incubation commences, and moving a few pieces of timber around outside the tree would not have disturbed them in any way; however, if she was merely roosting in the hole during the day she may not have felt as tolerant. I would need to wait until I had strong evidence that there were eggs in the nest hole, which normally would not be the case until early/mid-May – but this pair obviously didn't follow the crowd.

I returned to the woodland on 20 April after an absence of ten days. It was late afternoon, and spring was finally advancing after a slow start. The woodland floor was turning a light shade of green as carpets of wood anemone and wood sorrel began unfurling and spreading along the ground. The first house martins were flying overhead, twittering excitedly as they headed up the valley, northbound with the spring. Summer migrants, including willow warbler, chiffchaff and blackcap, were well-represented in the woodland chorus, alongside our resident thrushes and finches.

As I approached the clearing, a woodpecker flew silently away from the top of the nest tree. I positioned myself under the holly tree again, but this time I must have been still visible to keen eyes, as after a short period of time the male woodpecker arrived on an overhead branch, calling agitatedly and looking down at me. There was no sign of the female peering out of the nest hole at all during this commotion, which suggested that maybe he was waiting to go in – if only this annoying two-legged predator would go away first.

Taking the unsubtle hint, I slowly moved another 100m back into the woodland, all the time keeping my eye on both the nest tree and the male woodpecker high up in the leafless canopy. When finally I found a convenient log on which to sit, I realised that the male had stopped calling. I watched the nest hole through my binoculars and, a few seconds later, a woodpecker flew directly into the hole and disappeared from view. Moments later, the male stuck his head out and looked around, reassuring himself that all was well before going back inside. He looked out again a few moments later as he shuffled around before finally settling down. It was only 17.30 so he wasn't preparing to roost – he was beginning to incubate. It was only the 20 April, and already the eggs had been laid – it was going to be an early season.

Now that the nest contained eggs, I knew it would be safe to put together my hide, enabling me to watch the birds at relatively close range and, most importantly, without disturbing them. I had already measured the distance between the two trees, which lay north-east of the nest, since effectively I intended using them as corner posts. They were quite close together, unfortunately, so the hide would have to be quite narrow, but there seemed to be no other trees I could use without undertaking a large and potentially disturbance-filled construction project. I decided the quickest and most practical solution was to try to use towels as sides and backs, since they could simply be pinned to the trees and trimmed quickly with scissors, far preferable to having to cut pieces of timber to size with a saw.

The following morning, I arrived shortly after 08.30. I fixed a beam across the two trees, about one metre high, and attached a piece of hardboard to this, creating a front screen into which I then cut observation holes at suitable heights and in different directions. Using a number of large towels to form the sides and back, and another piece of hardboard balancing on a fence post to create a roof, I created a practical, albeit very cramped, viewing hide in under half an hour. As

I had precut all of the timber I was using and had predrilled holes for the screws, I didn't need to use any power tools: I simply attached the temporary fittings to the trees with my Swiss Army knife.

I was putting in the final few screws when I heard a woodpecker call about fifty metres away. I quickly went into the hide, closed the curtain behind me and waited. I looked through the small hole I had made in the front, just wide enough for my binoculars. As I watched, the male woodpecker arrived on the tree just below the entrance hole, and as soon as the female had flown off, he went into the nest and settled down – either unaware or unperturbed by my presence.

I knew from the British Trust for Ornithology that great spotted woodpeckers in Great Britain incubate for fourteen to sixteen days. Although I had no way of knowing when the eggs had been laid, I suspected that, given that 20 April was so early in the season, they couldn't really have been incubating for more than a day or two. If the 20th were day one of incubation then I could expect the eggs to hatch between 4 and 6 May. However, I thought it unlikely that I had witnessed the actual first day of incubation; more likely it was day two or day three. Therefore, I expected that chicks would be hatching in the first few days of May, but possibly as early as the last day or two of April.

The following morning brought the first swallows back from Africa, the true harbingers of spring. As I made my way along the river to the hide, they twittered above me as they flew over my head, before skimming over the treetops and on to their next destination. Reaching the hide I was greeted with silence – no woodpeckers called to herald my arrival. Perhaps they hadn't started incubating after all? Stashing my telescope and rucksack in the corner of the hide, I watched through the openings for any signs of activity. Almost twenty minutes had passed without sign of the birds when a movement at the nest hole caught my attention. There, looking out from the hole and as quiet as could be, was the male woodpecker. He looked around the glade for about twenty seconds before satisfying himself all was well and retreating back inside to continue his parental duties. Pulling out my flask and biscuits, I made myself comfortable for the day ahead.

My flask contained neither tea nor coffee but simply hot water, as I cannot abide the taste of either 'stewed tea' or 'stewed coffee' that has been kept in a flask for hours on end. While I have a definite preference for freshly brewed ground coffee, the complexities of making it amongst the trees meant that my woodland tipple was tea. Only Barry's *Gold Blend* was good enough for this setting, accompanied by a packet of McVitie's *Chocolate Hobnobs*. Watching birds and animals in their natural habit takes time, and it is always best to be prepared for a long stay. Being cold and hungry does little to enhance the experience and both my flask and packet of *Chocolate Hobnobs* were invariably empty at the end of each day!

I was sitting there in the hide watching the trees in front of me as the male sat inside the tree, incubating, when I heard 'music'. Distantly at first, a melodious yodelling which gradually developed into the sound of baying foxhounds as they followed their quarry's scent, but the cries of these hounds were coming not from the nearby fields or woods in front of me, they were coming from the sky. One of the most beautiful sounds in Ireland, evoking both wildness and loneliness, it was one I knew well. These were the cries of the greenland white-fronted goose... and they were on their way home.

Ireland is the winter home to over half of the world's population of these geese, most of which spend their time here on the reclaimed sloblands of the Wexford Wildfowl Reserve. From a world population of almost 19,000 birds, 8,000 spend the winter there, with another couple of thousand birds distributed across the lakes and bogs of the Irish midlands.

I climbed out from the hide and looked upwards as the cries of these 'hounds of the sky' steadily increased in volume. The open expanse of the sky was marred by a network of boughs and branches and gradually emerging foliage, which obscured much of the vista. Worried that I would miss them and with their clamouring cries reaching a crescendo as they neared overhead, I quickly ran across the glade to where there was an opening in the canopy. And there, over the highest oaks, at a considerable height, was a skein of geese. Flying in broad V formation, they were headed by a single bird, which was almost certainly an experienced adult who would have made this journey on several occasions and knew the way, safely leading the less experienced younger birds. Their cries, so much like baying dogs that wildfowlers have often referred to them as 'Heaven's Hounds', filled the air as they passed overhead. They were travelling generally in a north-westerly direction that would take them from Wexford through the glaciated valleys of Wicklow and across the great central plain of the Irish midlands until they reached the Donegal coast. From there, without stopping, they would cross the sea until they reached Iceland, where they would rest before carrying on over the Greenland Ice Cap to their breeding grounds in the Arctic Tundra.

Despite the musical and uplifting sounds that filtered down from the passing skein, I was saddened watching them pass over and start to disappear into the distance. They were travelling to a land that had held a fascination for me since I was a boy; the wild Arctic landscape which had claimed so many explorers' lives and the vast, open expanses of which were home to a host of fascinating creatures, none of which I would ever see... how I wished I could follow those birds on their wonderful voyage.

Their yodelling cries had faded and I was still standing there watching the sky when I heard a *Kik* from the trees nearby: the female woodpecker was returning to relieve her mate, so I returned to my hide.

Unfortunately, I was going to be absent from the area for at least a week, if not more. I was immensely disappointed, but there was no way to avoid it, I hadn't expected the woodpeckers to be incubating so early. The only consolation I offered myself was that activity is normally quite minimal during incubation compared to when the chicks hatch. All things considered, this was probably the better of the two periods during which to be missing. I was certain of one thing however, on my return, I expected to be very busy. My hide was up, the birds were incubating and the stage was set for an exciting show.

I returned to the woodland on 1 May and was amazed to see how the woodland had changed in such a short period. The beech trees had exploded into leaf, flooding the woodland below in a suffuse green light that seemed almost ethereal. Emergent beech leaves are soft and semi-transparent, and the light filtering through them makes a beech woodland one of the most enchanting habitats to explore for those few short weeks during which the leaves first appear. By June the leaves are no longer soft but have hardened and become opaque, shading the ground beneath.

The summer chorus was in full song. Blackcaps and whitethroats, both fresh in from Africa, were singing from the scrubland and woodland edges, competing with dunnocks, wrens, blackbirds and song thrushes. Spotted flycatchers, usually the last of our summer migrants to arrive from Africa, were giving their insect-like song of clicks and wheezes. Ravens gruffly 'croaked' overhead as their brood of youngsters took their first faltering flaps from their nest in the high oaks, joining the myriad swallows that were hawking for insects over the treetops. Early summer is such a magical season, filled with wondrous and unique sights and sounds of nature, and I firmly believe that time should be set aside to enjoy this season more than any other.

I arrived at the hide and quickly went inside; there were no calls from the woodpeckers to indicate that I had been spotted. I sat quietly in the hide and quickly realised that while it was practical, it was extremely cramped and uncomfortable, with no room for any sort of seat or support. I watched the nest hole, wondering if all was well after my absence; anything could have happened to my woodpeckers and I would have been none the wiser.

I need not have worried though. After about fifteen minutes, a small black and white head peered out from the nest hole and looked around. I caught a flash of red as the head turned, and I knew then it was the male. After satisfying himself that all was well, he went back in to brood his eggs, or possibly his young if they had already hatched. It is a curious thing about brooding woodpeckers that, every once in a while, the bird that is incubating will, for no apparent reason, leave the eggs and climb up to the entrance hole and look out. They never seem alarmed when doing this, and often close their eyes as though dozing while sitting there. Why they do this is unknown. It could be to look and see if the mate is nearby or to check for predators, yet why would you alert a predator to the presence of a nest by sticking your head out of a nest hole? I have never seen blackbirds, robins or blue tits leave the eggs just to have a 'look-see'. Perhaps the effort of sitting for prolonged periods in the darkness and confinement of the nest chamber for a couple of weeks is something that even birds find challenging, and they simply need to get a breath of fresh air without entirely neglecting their duties.

After about fifteen minutes, the female arrived quietly just below the nest hole. A moment later, the male flew out of the hole and into the canopy while the female quickly went inside to take his place. Although the changeover had been typically fast, I had had sufficient time to confirm that she did not have food in her bill when she arrived, definitively confirming that no chicks had hatched yet – I had made it back in time.

The weather in early May is often glorious in Wicklow, and this year was no exception. The sun spent its allocated time each day in a seemingly infinite azure sky, with the only interruption being the occasional wisps of cirrus mares' tails, galloping over 6,000m above the spanish chestnut tree where my woodpeckers patiently maintained a constant vigil over their eggs. The days passed and there was still no sign of food being brought to the nest.

The pattern of activity during incubation is quite constant. Both the male and female take turns incubating, regardless of the size of the clutch. Eggs are brooded constantly and rarely left unattended, unlike with some other species where brooding is carried out solely by one of the sexes. The male and female changed places about once every thirty minutes, allowing the other to feed and exercise. The actual changeover is always fascinating to watch from the setting of a hide. I had previously watched many changeovers at other nests where I had not used a hide but instead watched from a distance using a telescope. Even so, the bird arriving to the nest hole would invariably spot me sitting alone in the distance and would call several times before approaching the nest. However, when I was concealed in the hide, the birds' approach was usually silent, unannounced and sudden.

Without warning, the female would usually land directly below the nest hole, her head tilted slightly back as she eyed the surrounding woodland for any sign of predators. She was so closely positioned to the nest hole that the tip of her bill was almost level with the bottom edge of the nest hole. The male, sitting alone in the dark inside the nesting chamber, was unable to see her arrival, nor would he even know when to expect it, yet the moment he heard her alight on the bark outside he would be gone, like a rat out of a bolthole, flying up into the sunlit canopy. The speed with which he emerged was always impressive – his breast feathers seemed to barely miss the upturned bill of the female below him as he flew out. Rather than simply emerging, he seemed to explode from the nest hole with such force that it was as though he could not wait to get away from the world of darkness he had endured for the previous half hour. Each time he exited the hole, he would give a distinctive low chuckling call as he flew past the female. It was a similar sound to that which the birds often gave during their nuptial flights, only considerably lower in pitch. If I hadn't been sitting so close to the nest in the hide, it may even have gone unnoticed. I never heard the female make any call when she exited the nest hole, but the male did so on almost every occasion I witnessed him leaving during incubation, although he completely ceased this behaviour later in the season when the young had hatched. He would only barely have flown past the female when she would quickly squeeze herself into the nest hole, shaking her tail from side to side as she did so. This all happened so fast and was so choreographed that she would almost be sitting on the eggs before he had landed in the canopy. Later on in the season, whenever they came out of the nest hole, the parents often stayed around the tree preening. However, during incubation they kept the activity there to an absolute minimum to avoid drawing attention to the nest.

When the male returned to relieve the female, he would often call distantly beforehand. It was because of this habit of foretelling his arrival that I usually tried to write my notes, open my Thermos or excavate my knapsack in the vain hope of finding another Mars bar during the time he was away from the nest. The faint *kik* was enough notice to make me stop what I was doing and refocus on the job in hand. As I scanned the canopy, minutes passed in silence before I glimpsed him flying silently through the treetops and alighting on the topmost branches near the edge of the glade. From there, satisfied that there was no danger, he would glide to one of the neighbouring trees on outstretched wings, landing about halfway down the length of the trunk. Only then, if completely satisfied all was well, would he silently fly to the nest hole. The sound of his claws scratching on the bark and the noise of his wings as he landed were all that told the female of his arrival, and her silent departure to the canopy was equally as rapid as his. As he shuffled into the nest hole, he almost appeared to have got stuck as his tail remained sticking out of the nest hole longer than usual. Most likely, he was using his bill to turn the eggs around before settling down onto them, since this would be almost impossible to do when sitting in the confines of the tree. A moment later the tail disappeared, leaving me to sit there awaiting the female's return.

The day passed with the hour marked by the sun and the half hour marked by the woodpeckers. As the sun moved further west, I left the woodland and the woodpeckers to their repetitive routine. I returned the following morning, 2 May, and settled into the hide; no woodpecker had heralded my arrival and I had no idea which of the pair was incubating. After a few minutes had passed, and as usual without notice, the female appeared below the nest hole; however this time she looked different...her bill seemed thicker. I reached for my binoculars as the male sped past her, chuckling his way into the canopy like a feathered hyena, and quickly focused them on the female before she disappeared inside the tree. Her bill wasn't thicker; it was partially open because she was carrying food...

The chicks had finally hatched.

4.
NEW LIFE

IT WAS THIRTEEN DAYS since I had seen the male looking out from the nest hole. Given that woodpeckers usually incubate for fourteen to sixteen days, the eggs had obviously been laid in the days prior to my watching the bird on the 20 April. Despite being a widespread species in global terms, and one that is relatively easily watched at the nest, its habit of nesting deep inside a tree means that several aspects of its ecology are not well-documented. One of these concerns whether or not all of the eggs in a clutch hatch on the same day, as with some hole nesters such as blue tits, or whether they hatch over a series of days, as with other hole-nesting species such as barn owls. The variation amongst species is down to when incubation actually starts. Most birds lay one egg each day but some species only start incubation once the clutch is complete, resulting in all the eggs hatching on the same day, whereas others start incubating as soon as the first egg is laid, which results in hatching being staggered over several days.

In previous years when I watched young woodpeckers in the days before leaving the nest, some seemed more developed than others. This strongly suggested to me that they were of different ages, the brood having hatched over several days, but the differences were not as marked as I would have expected had some birds been four or five days older than their siblings. I had always felt that woodpeckers did not fit either model, but rather were 'fluid'. Because the adults roost in the nest hole, the first-laid eggs would benefit from the resulting extra warmth in the chamber before active incubation commenced following the laying of the final egg. This would explain the slight variation in ages I often noted at the nest hole. If this was the case then I believed it was quite likely that only some of the chicks had hatched that day and that the rest would hatch the following day or even as late as the day after that. Unfortunately, I had no way of knowing the brood size – there could be anywhere between three and seven chicks. In Great Britain the normal brood size averages five, and although one nest in Ireland had been confirmed to contain five chicks, many broods I have watched develop seem to regularly only have two or three.

The day that the first chicks hatched out was as perfect a day as you could wish for; the sun, its rays now starting to be filtered by the vibrant emerald green of the softly unfolding beech trees, lit up the nest hole like a stage light awaiting the next scene – and that scene unfolded with great speed. The days of quietly watching the continuous brooding, with little activity to observe other than the clockwork-like changeovers every half hour or so, were now replaced with a scale of activity almost frantic by comparison.

Newly-hatched woodpeckers emerge naked, with no feathers to provide insulating warmth, so they still require continuous brooding during those first days of life, until such time as their feathers begin to grow. This means that only one of the parents can forage for food while the other remains at the nest. The parent-bird gathering food usually returns within about ten minutes of having left the nest, and the brooding bird will then leave the chamber to allow its mate to enter. After feeding the young, it then remains to brood them until its partner returns, beginning the cycle again.

With my spanish chestnut woodpeckers, it was interesting to see that no matter which of the pair was out foraging, it would invariably return on average after ten minutes; this seemed to be the length of time that was required to find a bill-full of food of the right size. Later on, after a couple of weeks, the visits became a lot less regular and seemed to be regulated by the food source being exploited at the time. Thanks to the proximity of my hide to the nest, and by using my telescope, it was possible to see the type of food being collected. Naturally, since the newly-hatched chicks were so tiny, the food provided was small enough to be placed into their waiting mouths.

The small portions being served by the parents at mealtimes often made it challenging to see what they were being fed. Unlike the changeovers I had observed during incubation, when the returning bird would fly straight to the nest hole and almost have to duck to avoid being hit by the exiting bird, now the returning birds landed further down the tree and well below the nest hole entrance. The female, in particular, often flew from the canopy, gliding on outstretched wings like a giant flying squirrel in the jungles of South East Asia, to land on the side of the tree, about two-thirds of a metre below the entrance hole. She would look around and slowly make her way obliquely up the trunk with an almost hesitant motion, before pausing at the entrance hole. The male, hearing her movements on the bark, would exit the nest hole upon her approach. Her stationary pose at the entrance hole would then give me a chance to study what she was carrying in her bill.

Sometimes the contents were white: undoubtedly the larvae of the numerous wood-boring beetles that reside in the decaying timber which permeate the surrounding woodland. These larvae come in a variety of sizes, depending on both age and species. Presumably whenever she excavated large larvae, which would be too large for her newly-hatched chicks to swallow, she would consume them herself.

At other times, she would arrive with a bill full of dark food, and numerous small legs could sometimes be glimpsed protruding like nasal hairs. These were most likely flying insects or spiders gathered from amongst the often still bare canopy where they would sit basking in the early summer sunshine. I have never seen an adult woodpecker availing of this food source at other times of the year and have often wondered if they only forage for this protein-rich food when providing for fast-growing youngsters. This is not unusual amongst birds and a very notable example of this behaviour is exhibited by the waxwing.

The waxwing is without doubt the most exotic-looking visitor one can hope to see in Ireland. When they arrive, it is the most eagerly awaited highlight of a birdwatcher's winter – if they arrive. They are not a regular visitor and sometimes several years pass by with no sightings anywhere in the country, only for hundreds of birds to be seen in a subsequent year. Breeding in the extensive boreal band of trees which surrounds the Arctic Circle, they irrupt south in the autumn to feed on the rich berry crops which populate Europe, swarming into our parks and gardens and gorging themselves on the scarlet rowan and cotoneaster berries, which are such a feature of the suburbs of our cities. A palette of colour like no other graces this species: shades of pink, yellow, chestnut, scarlet and ash, grey scream in garish contrast, yet blend harmoniously into one of nature's finest sights.

As the winter wanes and the sun returns above the horizon in the frozen north, these colourful travellers return to their boreal origins to raise their families. And having spent the preceding six months gorging almost to capacity on fruits and berries, they now feed themselves and rear their young solely on insects. They do so because berries would not be readily available in their northern breeding grounds until later in the season. Even if they could obtain them, the protein content of most berries is not sufficient to support rapidly developing chicks. Whether or not there is much variation in the protein levels between wood-boring beetle larvae and various other insects I am unable to say, but flying insects do seem to make up a considerable portion of a young woodpecker's early diet, a fact borne out by the bird sitting in front me.

The female great spotted woodpecker continued to look around the glade in which I sat, her small beady eye checking for anything out of the ordinary. Finally, having satisfied herself that all was as it should be, she squeezed her body into the cavity and fed the youngsters before settling down to brood while awaiting the male's return.

Watching woodpeckers squeezing themselves into the nest hole always fascinates me. They make the hole the absolute bare minimum diameter that will allow them to just about fit their bodies into, a survival strategy many hole-nesting species use to ensure no predator larger than themselves can follow. However, I often felt they could make it a fraction larger to allow them a bit more comfort during the approximate thousand times they each must pass through! Their heads and shoulders, being more streamlined and bullet shaped, flow through the entrance with ease; then, the bird seems momentarily to hesitate as the broadest part of its back seals the entrance like a cork in a bottle. By shaking and waggling its tail from side to side, like a spawning salmon thrusting itself up a weir, it generates the momentum required to get inside. The final sight it affords to an observer before disappearing is its vibrant scarlet undertail melting into the darkness. Seen from behind, as was my view from where I sat in the hide, it is an unusual perspective, since the woodpecker's body forms an oval, being broader than it is high, like a slightly flattened tennis ball.

Throughout the rest of that day, the birds maintained a regular visiting schedule, with little deviation from the ten minute routine. There was little to disturb the new family in the spanish chestnut tree and the glade was peaceful as evening approached and signalled the end of their first day as a true family.

As I made my way back along the banks of the Avonmore River, the setting sun brought a drop in temperature, as is often the case in the Wicklow Mountains during May. Traditionally May is the first month of summer, and at lower elevations this may hold true. There the lush growth along the verges, combined with hedgerows bedecked in pink and white hawthorn blossom, shout summer for all those with eyes to see and noses to smell. Nevertheless, here in the

Discovering the natural world around us

Feeding marks made by a great spotted woodpecker

A distinctive row of 'feeding-pits' made by a great spotted woodpecker

The male great spotted woodpecker is a strikingly handsome bird, boldly plumaged in black and white with a splash of red

The female great spotted woodpecker lacks the red spot on the back of the head, but otherwise her plumage is identical to that of the male

During incubation, the male often looked out of the nest hole before settling down to brood the eggs

The pair took turns at incubating the eggs, changing places once every half-hour

The parents would arrive with food for the newly-hatched chicks about once every ten minutes

Great spotted woodpeckers are fastidious housekeepers, removing each faecal sac as soon as it is produced by a chick

Young great spotted woodpeckers often have a completely red crown. Their stubby bills and muted face pattern combine to give them an endearingly cute appearance

In the final days before leaving the nest, the youngsters spend much of their time at the entrance hole, looking out at the world beyond

Using its tail for support on a peanut feeder, a great spotted woodpecker has a distinctive banana shape

The winter woodland habitat of the great spotted woodpecker

... is a lifetime's journey

Wicklow Mountains, true summer was at least a month away and 'May blossom', as Hawthorn flowers are often called, would have to wait. Faint wisps of evening mist rose from the river as I reflected on the day's events; once again this pair of woodpeckers had hatched their young well in advance of all the other pairs scattered throughout the woodlands in the surrounding district. Some of the neighbouring pairs might not even start incubation for a couple of weeks and most pairs would only be laying their final egg in the coming days, yet this pair were now feeding young; why so early? What was it that made this pair so different and stand out from their peers? The question nagged at me continuously, like an aching thorn in the flesh, yet the answer continued to elude me.

I returned the following day and my arrival was greeted with a loud *KIK*. I was a couple of hundred metres from the hide and I had unexpectedly met the male. He was on a small oak tree in front of me, hacking his way into a partly rotten spur; small chips of wood lay scattered on the ground below him – he wasn't the tidiest of carpenters. He called again before flying down along the track away from the nest. I quickly ran up to the tree, and seeing no sign of the female, I moved past and made my way into the hide. Moments later a head peered out and looked around, as though she had heard something but wasn't quite sure what it was or whether it represented a threat. Thanks to my hide, my presence went undetected, and having reassured herself that there was no imminent threat, she disappeared back inside.

It was day two of the new family and my main thought was how large the brood was going to be and how many youngsters I would be able to identify by their head patterns when they started to come up to the entrance hole to be fed in a couple of weeks' time. I was pondering on this when the male returned, landing high on the tree where the main trunk gave way to a single remaining decaying bough. He stayed there for a few moments, the morning sun catching the whiteness of his underparts and rendering them a suffuse yellow. After a quick preen he flew down to the lower trunk, whereupon the female emerged to allow him to enter. This time she didn't fly off, but rather hopped slightly to one side while he hopped up the tree until he was level with her on the far side of the hole. It was the first time I had seen them sitting alongside each other at the entrance hole, like two proud parents, while their offspring lay inside. The male had returned without food, so his foraging on this occasion had seemingly been for his own benefit. Nevertheless, after a brief shared moment with his partner, he moved into the nest hole and the female flew quietly into the canopy.

It was far more overcast that morning than it had been the day before and the calm conditions that prevailed had enticed the first emergence of Wicklow's infamous biting midge. While officially it is known as *Culicoides impunctatus,* it is usually referred to in far simpler words, none of which are complimentary to say the least. This tiny insect, only a couple of millimetres in length, has a bite completely out of proportion to its size and one which can cause misery to humans and animals alike. In past years, nothing had hindered my woodpecker observations at nests more than these persistent little nippers. Minutes after I would sit down in a woodland to watch a nest, they would begin to seek me out, crawling through my hair to reach my scalp. Swarming over my eyelids and into my ears they would bite and bite until I could stand it no longer. After no more than ten minutes I would be forced to beat a hasty, sweaty and madly itching retreat back through the woods, cursing and swearing and wishing God hadn't created such a seemingly pointless lifeform!

By watching the woodpeckers from my hide all this misery was avoided, as although the midges had fought for my life's blood as I made my way along the river, they never sought me out when positioned inside. Without this shelter it would have been impossible for me to endure the endless hours required to watch the family grow. Although the midges had been absent during the previous month, their daily emergence from this point onwards would result in the woodlands throughout the Wicklow Mountains being inundated by countless billions of these tiny insects.

Ten minutes had now passed without any sign of the female returning to the nest. Then, unexpectedly, the male looked out from within the nest hole, peering first around the glade and then upwards at the overcast sky with his beady eye. Woodpeckers, more than any other bird I have watched, can appear very reptilian as they look out from their nest holes. When doing so they stretch out their necks making them long and sinuous in appearance, which, when combined with their large staring eyes and streamlined bills, all add to the serpentine appearance.

He disappeared from view, only to poke his head out again a few seconds later, this time with something white held gently in his bill. At first I thought it was a faecal sac[7] produced by the chicks, but it was too white and had a smooth shiny appearance that no faecal sac would display; it was an eggshell.

I looked carefully through my binoculars and could make out the sharply defined edges that framed this piece of hard calcium carbonate, which until a short while beforehand had encased a small woodpecker. The male seemed uncertain as to what to do next and continued to look around the glade. His instinct was to carry the shell away from the nest, since simply to drop it outside at the foot of the tree could draw unwelcome attention to the fact that there were chicks in the nest. However, with at least two naked chicks beneath him he was reluctant to leave without the female being on hand to take over his duties. Then came a *KIK* from the canopy above me and the male, in response, flew out from the nest hole carrying the eggshell into the trees. Within seconds the female, her bill full of food, had flown down to the nest hole and disappeared inside.

During that first week after the young woodpeckers hatched, there was little indication to anyone passing through the glade that a nest was present. The young were too small to begin climbing up to the nest hole as they would do when older; they were also silent during

---

7 Faecal sac: A mucous/gelatinous membrane encasing the waste products excreted by the chick.

that first week, unlike the cacophonous chorus that would emanate from this tree in the weeks to follow. Only the parents' ceaseless and clockwork-like to-ing and fro-ing throughout the day gave any indication of the youngsters' presence.

From where I watched, outside, it was impossible to see exactly what was going on inside the tree; but that didn't mean I was completely unaware of what was happening to the chicks during that first week – after all I wasn't the first person to be fascinated with this species. It was during the late 1950s that many insights were revealed into this stage of a woodpecker's life, and it is thanks to the innovative observations made by Heinz Sielmann[8] that we know what happens during this first week of their life.

Having located great spotted woodpecker nests in Bavaria, Sielmann would wait until the eggs had hatched and would then carefully remove the back of the trunk to expose the full nest cavity. He then sealed off the exposed nest chamber with a clear plastic panel, and a canvas hide containing a cine camera was then built onto a platform, which had been fitted against the tree. All of this took place on scaffolding, which had been erected to access the nest, which was situated ten metres above the ground. Amazingly, the parents were not bothered by this and carried on feeding the young throughout this invasion of their privacy. Once in place, he was able to film the lives of the chicks from inside the nest when they were no more than a few days old; although now well over half a century old, the black and white film footage he obtained has never been replicated.

The bottom of the nest cavity was shown to be completely bare, devoid of any nesting material that might offer warmth to the naked nestlings. A few loose wood chips, left over from when the parents had excavated the chamber, lay scattered around. However, rather than deliberately being arranged so as to provide a lining, as was often thought to be the case, they gave the appearance of having been left behind as the parents cleared out the chamber. This was consistent with

---

8 My Year with the Woodpeckers by Heinz Sielmann.

what I had found myself when examining nest holes during wintertime when they were not in use. Using a handheld flexible exploration camera, I had examined the bottom of the nesting chambers and never found any indication of any attempt to line a nest with wood chips. Because of this stark, almost barren, environment they have emerged into, the chicks huddle together for warmth when they are not being brooded by their parents.

During those first few days, they sit in a tight clump in the centre of the chamber, their bills pointing skyward, their eyes still not yet open. As the days pass, their feathers start to grow and begin covering their pink bodies. This normally happens by around day five, about the same time as their eyes open. Normally, the opening of a young bird's eyes enables it to see the world around it, but there is very little for the young woodpeckers to see in the darkness of the chamber, save for a small circle of light high above them. I knew from the previous use of my exploration camera that very little light from the entrance hole penetrates to the bottom of the chamber and that the young woodpecker's first ten days are spent in almost complete darkness. By the end of the first week, they have sufficient feathering that they do not need to be continuously brooded for warmth, and both parents can now forage for food simultaneously. While waiting for food, the chicks continue to sit in a pyramidal heap, but often the strongest of the brood will sit on top of the others so as to reach the returning parent first.

When the parent bird returns it usually feeds just one chick per visit, rather than dividing the food equally amongst the siblings; invariably the strongest bird, usually the first hatched, will be fed until fully sated, whereupon it will fall asleep allowing its less dominant siblings to feed unchallenged. The neck muscles of newly-hatched woodpeckers are not strong enough at first to allow them to keep their heads aloft and the returning adult bird has to present the food to its offspring by pressing its bill against their bodies to encourage them to open their bills weakly, allowing the parent to place the food inside. By the end of the first week, the chicks eagerly greet the parent upon his or her return and the parent simply has to feed the chick on top of the pile.

Having fed the chick, the parent then turns its attention to its tiny charge's bodily motions; by gently pressing against the chick's bottom it encourages it to pass a faecal sac containing digested food remains. It gently removes this from the chick and takes it out of the nest. Woodpeckers are fastidiously houseproud and nest chambers examined by camera during the winter months have been shown to be spotless with not a single faecal waste sack left behind despite the young spending over three weeks in the nest. Other hole-nesting species are rather less fastidious in their property maintenance, and some species are so lax that they border on disgusting. The hoopoe is one such bird.

The hoopoe is an exotic and rare visitor to Ireland from Africa and the Mediterranean. A striking bird, about the size of a thrush, it is pink with black and white zebra-striped wings and a crest like that of a Native American chief, which it can raise and lower at will. Sadly, the small numbers which are recorded in Ireland each spring, having accidentally flown too far north from their African wintering grounds, never remain to nest and instead return to their breeding grounds. This is a great pity as a pair of these exotic beauties in an Irish woodland would certainly be a sight worth seeing. Like the woodpecker, they nest in holes in trees, but unlike the woodpecker they use naturally occurring cavities rather than excavate their own. For reasons known only to them, they make no attempt to remove their youngsters' faeces from the nest, and by the time their brood is ready to leave they are sitting on three weeks' worth of family excrement, the smell of which can be detected several metres away.

Throughout that first week after the woodpecker chicks hatched, the glade had remained relatively silent, other than for the periodic warning calls the parents gave to signal my arrival or departure. But by the week's end, a new sound had emerged to join the rich and varied soundscape that surrounded me: a gentle soft 'purring', which would rise and fall in both volume and pitch, now emanated from the tree with a slow and steady rhythm. This purring is the first of several distinct phases through which the chicks begging calls pass before they leave the nest. As the chicks grow, the sounds they make gradually change until they are almost identical to those of an adult bird, which only occurs a day or two before they follow their parents out of the chamber and into the trees. Once one becomes familiar with the various sounds made by chicks at different stages of development, it becomes possible to estimate the age of unseen chicks in a nest, based purely on their vocalisations, and usually to be accurate to within a couple of days.

The gentle, almost soothing, sound which arrived at the end of the first week was clearly audible from where I sat in my hide watching the parents tending to the youngsters, and it formed a pleasant backdrop against which the activities of the parents could be observed. When only one parent was looking for food and the other brooded the chicks, the number of visits to the nest per hour had averaged around seven, or about once every eight-and-a-half minutes. Surprisingly, when both parents were out foraging, the frequency with which they returned with food remained the same; however, the quantity of food being brought to the nest with each visit substantially increased. The bills of the returning adult birds were crammed so full of multi-coloured insect mush that they reminded me of a pistachio nut, with the split shell revealing the green kernel inside.

It was now approaching the middle of May and the oak trees were finally unfurling their leaves. Oaks are the last of our native trees to come into leaf and a full oak canopy is not complete until early June. The ethereal jade-green light cast across the glade by the sunlight filtering through the almost transparent beech tree leaves was now being replaced by a darker, yellow-toned and far colder light, as the oak leaves increasingly shielded the woodland floor from the sun's rays. It was now becoming harder to watch the adult birds in the trees as they were often obscured by the leaves. During the preceding weeks, the distant call announcing a returning adult bird would have me scanning the treetops in the hope of glimpsing it gliding through the branches, whereas now I would simply focus on the nest hole itself. Otherwise, I could easily have missed the bird completely were I to waste time scanning the infinite mosaic of leaves above me. Because it was now almost impossible to follow them as they roamed through the woods, they often surprised me by appearing at unexpected times.

One afternoon I had watched the female leave the nest and fly into the treetops. From there she seemed to disappear as she flew into the trees beyond. I had just settled back into my seat when a loud tapping sounded from close by. However, try as I might, I couldn't locate the source. Despite my hide having viewing holes facing all directions, no matter what aspect of the woodland I viewed I could not see the bird making the noise, and yet still it continued ... tap... tap... tap... tap. I slowly pulled back the cloth screen that acted as a door at the back of the hide and pushed my head outside – and there, no more than 2m away from my nose, was the female woodpecker. She was perched on the buttresses of a neighbouring tree, at the bottom of the trunk, her tail almost touching the ground. She pecked away at the thick growth of moss that covered the bark and scarcely seemed to notice my unexpected appearance from behind the curtain. Having extracted a large white grub from its hiding place under the coarse bark, she flew up and into the nest hole.

It was now almost the end of the second week after hatching and the gentle purring sounds of the young woodpeckers had been replaced by a louder and more strident *keekeekeekeekeekeekee* which was just as endless as the purring sounds and also rose and fell in pitch, presumably as the youngsters turned their heads from side to side. I have always been intrigued as to why the young of so many hole-nesting species of bird tend to be so vocal. The purpose of nesting in a hole as opposed to simply in a hedge like a blackbird is obviously to give greater protection to the young from predators; so why then draw attention to the nest by having young that are so vocal? Starlings and Jackdaws are two other hole-nesting species with extremely noisy young, so it obviously is a trait shared by several hole-nesting species, rather than just woodpeckers alone.

While it is relatively simple to follow the sounds of young woodpeckers to the general vicinity of the nest, it can be surprisingly difficult to identify the exact tree in which the nest is located, especially if the entrance hole is concealed by an overhanging spur. Despite the sounds the young make, the acoustic properties of the nest chamber itself can offer some protection; the *keekeekee* calls of the young seem to come from everywhere and yet nowhere. The sound is audible from all four compass points and strangely is rarely more pronounced on the side of the tree containing the entrance hole. The sounds the youngsters make seem to resonate out through the sides and the back of the nest chamber as much as they travel out through the entrance hole itself. So, although an area of trees containing a woodpecker nest is often easily located by the constant calling of the young, both myself and other observers have often had to just sit and wait, while well-hidden, for a returning adult bird to reveal exactly where the nest is.

The woodpecker chicks were now half-grown and beginning to explore the walls of the nesting chamber like trainee rock climbers learning to climb. When one of the adult birds returned with food, the chicks would climb up and meet its parent as it entered the nest hole. No longer did the adults completely disappear from view while I watched from the hide; instead, their scarlet undertail and pied upperparts remained sticking out of the hole, pointing skyward like a rocket launcher, while the bird stretched its head and neck down into the chamber to meet the scrabbling young. From this point onwards, the adult birds usually only entered the nest completely when removing a faecal sac from one of the chicks, or late in the evening when settling down to brood the youngsters for the night.

With each passing day, the chicks grew stronger and clambered further up the inside chamber walls so that the parents had to stretch less and less into the depths of the tree. Finally the day came when the first chick reached the entrance hole and was visible from where I sat, watching through my binoculars. To say he was visible is probably being generous; a nebulous shape was just about discernible in the darkest recesses of the nest hole behind the parent bird's head whilst being fed. These initial glimpses of the young were always tantalising as so little could be seen, the parent bird's head obscuring almost completely the moving shadow in the background. As soon as the chick had taken the food from the adult, it would retreat back into the cavity before the parent flew off. I often felt that perhaps their leg muscles were not yet strong enough to enable them to stay any longer than necessary. Although the entrance hole faced away from the sun for most of the day, keeping it in continuous shadow, I knew that for a brief minute or two the late evening rays usually shone directly into the cavity; in the same manner, the sunrise would light up the inner chamber of the Newgrange passage tomb on the winter solstice. The chick, or chicks, as I had yet to determine how many were in the nest, continued to come up to the nest hole for feeding throughout the day, and it was interesting to see how the parents adapted their feeding technique. They now had to turn their heads sideways as they passed the food from their bills into those of their frantically calling youngsters. The loudness of the chicks' calls had now increased, since they were climbing up to the entrance and projecting it out into the open woods. It had also changed in rhythm: instead of the continuous *KeeKeeKeeKee...* the calls were now being spaced *Kee... Kee... Kee... Kee...* almost as though the chick needed a breath to produce the increased volume.

By now the sun was sinking fast towards the western horizon, causing the mountains that formed that horizon to turn from the daylight hues of brown and green to the darker blue of approaching twilight. The rays of the setting sun moved along the bark of the spanish chestnut until they lit up the nest hole, and the usually infinite darkness of the entrance was replaced by the pale amber of the heartwood, which formed the back of the chamber.

Then, as though waiting in the wings for the stage lighting to commence, the male alighted on the tree just to the left of the nest hole. The sun reflected off the crimson on the back of his head, making it appear almost to glisten; it had the same hue and vibrancy as a drop of fresh blood. Sensing its father's return, a chick scaled the inner walls of the chamber and appeared at the nest hole, now fully lit by the last of the day's light, for a brief moment before being partially obscured by the male. A scarlet crown blazed across this young bird's forehead, extending from just before its eye to just past the midpoint of its crown. This red forehead and crown is found only on young woodpeckers and varies enormously; I have seen some young birds with a completely black crown, others with a full scarlet crown and many variations between; from a single red feather to several forming a neat red spot on the forehead. In years past, the chicks that have fledged from this particular territory have shown predominantly black heads. In fact, this individual sported the most red I had seen on any bird reared in the spanish chestnut tree. All too soon, the chick was sated and retreated back into the returning shadow of the nest hole, leaving the male to have a quick preen in the last rays of the setting sun, which moments later disappeared from view. With a loud *KIK* he flew away from the tree into the now darkening wood ...

The sun sank behind the Wicklow Mountains, which were black against the orange glow of the sky, and a silence settled on the glade.

5 ·
INTO THE UNKNOWN

THE PRECISE MOMENT that a young bird will leave the nest is very hard to predict and the odds are usually against an observer actually being present when it happens. However, it is one of the biggest moments in its life and one of the most rewarding to watch if you are fortunate enough to witness it. What triggers the urge to take that leap of faith is a mystery and when you consider it from the youngster's point of view, what is the benefit of doing it? He is safe, warm and food seems to be in endless supply, so why take this step into the unknown?

As far as we know, birds have very little, if any, ability to rationalise or consciously make decisions. The action of leaving the nest is thought to be governed by instincts, which have evolved to compel the chicks to leave. However, as I sat in the hide, I often wondered if it might be the simple amazement and excitement of the new world ahead of it that drives this urge?

A salmon that lives in a river must think that his world consists entirely of the immediate environment he sees around him, yet I wonder what must he think when he majestically leaps through the 'roof' of his world and discovers there is another world beyond his own? The excitement a young child feels when it snows and he wants to go outside to explore the magically altered landscape is made all the more powerful by his innocence. In the same way, does a young woodpecker, having lived in a twilight world for so many weeks, suddenly realise that by stepping though the portal of his world he enters an enchanted realm of light, colour and sound?

Whether it is really nothing other than simple instinct, something of which we have little comprehension, or the exciting possibilities of the new world calling to them, woodpecker chicks invariably leave the nest about three weeks after hatching.

As the chicks reach their third week in the nest, they spend more and more time at the entrance with their heads sticking out, calling for food. They are now almost the same size as their parents and only one chick at a time can look out, so they take turns clinging to the inside of the entrance hole as they await their parents' return. These last few days usually provide the best opportunities for estimating the number of young in the nest. Most field guide illustrations show juvenile great spotted woodpeckers with completely red crowns, extending from the base of the bill to the rear of the head. In Ireland at least, this extent of red is rarely shown and the amount of red on the crown usually extends no further than to the top of the head. In a number of cases, there is no red at all on the crown, which means that at a glance it can be hard to distinguish between some youngsters and their mother.

Having watched the heads sticking out for a whole day, I was satisfied that there were in fact only two birds in this brood. One had quite a bit of crimson on its crown whereas the other had only a small red thumbprint. I unceremoniously dubbed them 'Red' and 'Black'.

I was surprised that there were only two young, since most of the literature says that the brood size is usually between three and seven, with the average being five. However, over the years that I have watched woodpeckers both in this woodland and elsewhere in County Wicklow, the brood size as far as I can tell generally seems to average three, with four being reasonably regular. Although the species is well-established and has a firm foothold, perhaps the food supply in Ireland simply isn't sufficient to raise the larger broods typically recorded elsewhere in their range?

There was no way to tell from their behaviour whether Red and Black were male or female, since they would not acquire their adult plumage until the late autumn. However, their boisterous behaviour at the nest hole entrance, especially when being fed, reminded me very much of two young boys. But equally, they could both have been female.

Once Red and Black were eagerly looking out of the nest hole, I knew it would not be more than four or five days before they left, so I spent as much time as I could spare watching the nest from this point on. It quickly became apparent that Red was the more dominant of the two, and this raised the question, once more, of when do woodpeckers actually commence incubation? Almost all of our common songbirds lay one egg each day, usually early in the morning, until the clutch is complete, and only then will they start to incubate. This ensures that the eggs all hatch at the same time and that the birds all leave the nest together. However, some birds, such as the barn owl, will begin incubation as soon as the first egg in the clutch has been laid, so that the first chick might hatch four days before the final chick, giving the eldest sibling a good head start in life if food is short. I had always assumed that woodpeckers would only incubate when the clutch was complete, yet the development of these chicks, and many others I have seen, seems to be staggered, suggesting this is not the case. Frustratingly, without using a camera inside the nesting cavity, this is a puzzle that I am unlikely to resolve.

Red spent about three-quarters of his time sitting at the entrance hole, whereas Black spent significantly less. Only when Red's hunger was fully sated would he retire to the bottom of the nest cavity, allowing Black a chance to be fed. All the while that the young were at the entrance hole they kept up a continuous, almost endless, calling *kik... kik... kik... kik... kik... kik... kik* that seemed to rise and fall as they turned their heads to look around or to shuffle back into the nest cavity. Usually it was only the youngster at the entrance hole that was calling, so although the sound was often continuous as Red and Black swapped places at the entrance hole so too did they swap calling duties.

Sometimes Red would pause his calling and quizzically tilt his head to the side as though he was listening for his parents' return. Young woodpeckers spend the first few days of their final week in the nest clinging to the inside of the nest hole looking out. But as the days pass they gradually shift their focus and start gripping the nest entrance in a sitting position with their claws visible and their head perfectly framed by the nest opening. When they take up this position it is usually only about two days before they fly, and although they may look poised to jump at any minute they still have a bit of growing to do.

Red was so dominant when it came to feeding that I often wondered whether other siblings had succumbed to starvation before being old enough to climb up to the nest hole entrance and make their presence known to me. Sometimes I wouldn't see Black for an hour or so, and all the while Red would be sitting in front of the hole, calling constantly. When the parents returned to feed them, they would turn their heads sideways to allow the chicks to take the food from their bills. Red would be so enthusiastic that sometimes he would forget to let go of his parent's bill and an amusing tug-of-war would begin, with neither bird willing to let go.

The parents were now spending about sixteen hours a day feeding their chicks. Unfortunately, I was unable to follow their lives every minute of every day, but by varying my observation times I discovered that by late May, just before fledging, the parents were certainly feeding from at least 05.30 and most likely before that. They then fed the chicks pretty much continuously throughout the day, continuing to average about seven visits per hour. In the evening, the parents would feed up to around 21.00 but usually not too much beyond this. The youngsters were never amused by their parents' cessation of feeding, and one would often sit at the entrance hole calling impatiently until dusk began to fall, before grudgingly moving inside and settling down for the night. Even though they were almost fully grown by this stage, the father would still return each night to brood his youngsters, although how he managed to fit them both under his body is something I fail to understand. The male usually slipped quietly into the nest about half an hour before nightfall, around 22.00 at this time of year.

The purpose of brooding at this stage of the chick's development often puzzled me, as it was almost certainly nothing to do with providing warmth; given that the young by then were fully feathered and in no need of additional brooding. I suspected that the real purpose of such brooding was protection against predators. A few weeks later, in early June, I found out just how good woodpeckers were at defending their nest during the night. However, it involved both a different woodpecker family and a different nest.

The nest in question was several kilometres away, in different woodland but on the same river system. It was unusual in many respects – firstly, it was located less than 2m from ground level, making this the lowest nest I have ever seen. Secondly, it was in a natural cavity where a branch had broken off and rotted internally to form a vacant space with no woodpecker excavation of any sort having been carried out. Thirdly, the female bird was AWOL, possibly even dead, leaving the male with sole responsibility for feeding and brooding. Finally, and most unusually, there was only a single chick. It is probably a fair assumption that the original brood was larger but that the loss of the female resulted in the weaker chicks not receiving enough food and succumbing to hunger. Intriguingly, there were no dead chicks found in the nest when it was examined after the lone survivor had fledged, which raises the question whether the parents remove dead chicks from the nest. This tends not to occur in other hole-nesting species such as blue tits, and I have often found dead chicks in old nests when cleaning out nest boxes after birds have fledged.

I watched this unusual nest for several days. The chick was very close to fledging one morning, but unfortunately I had other engagements and had to leave him with his head sticking out, confident he would take to the wing later that day. It was the following evening when a friend and I returned. As expected, all was quiet with no sign of parent or chick. After half an hour of watching in vain, we walked on up the woods to look for roding[9] woodcock and to listen optimistically for the 'squeaking gate' calls of young long-eared owls.

On our return, in the gloaming, I decided to show my friend the nest hole up close, seeing as it was so low. We stood beside the tree, and with a torch I began to explain how the cavity had been naturally formed when, all of a sudden, I heard movement inside. I raised the torch and realised two things simultaneously – firstly, I could actually see completely inside the nest hole to the nest cavity, and secondly, the male bird was sitting there, astride the youngster – brooding. The male quickly realised that a 'predator' was looking in – he flattened his body against the chick, fanned his wings, craned his head around to face me and let loose the loudest, most incessant volley of *KIK... KIK... KIK... KIK...* I had ever heard. The noise at this proximity was absolutely deafening while the tone was undeniably aggressive and intimidating. Completely on instinct, I jumped back, dropping the torch, stumbled and landed on my back. The reason that the male woodpecker stayed in the nest each night until the chicks flew was simple; protection. If he had succeeded in driving me away, I felt it likely he would also succeed in driving away a pine marten or stoat.

Had I realised that the birds were still occupying the nest, I would never have approached it. Upon my return the following morning, I was glad to find that all was well and that the male was still feeding the chick. However, that afternoon, during my absence, the chick took flight. The last I saw of it was that same evening around 20.30, sitting high on the bough of a towering ancient oak, basking in the glow of the setting sun which bathed the wood in burnished gold – a picture of success.

---

[9] Roding: The crepuscular territorial display flight of the male woodcock.

Red and Black were more fortunate than that chick since they had both parents to care for them. The odds seemed to be stacked in their favour and by the end of May both youngsters seemed poised to leave the nest at any moment, weeks earlier than many of their neighbouring woodpecker families. Black still seemed a bit less keen than Red, however. The process of actually leaving the nest is a long and drawn-out one, and seems to be a stressful experience for both young and adults. Although many birds take their first flights early in the morning, with woodpeckers it can happen at any time of the day.

As the day approached when they would leave the nest, the parents seemed to have reached a stage which can only be described as 'being fed up'. Although they were still bringing food, it was clear that they felt it was time for the chicks to leave the nest. Their behaviour began to change as they spent more and more time enticing their youngsters to take that first step or, I should rather say, flight. The parents did this by bringing food to the nest as usual, but instead of feeding the chicks directly they remained a little distance away, just out of range unless the chick were to leave the nest hole.

This was fascinating to see, especially as not many bird species show this type of behaviour over such a protracted length of time. Several hole-nesting birds such as blue tits, starlings and house martins, often use enticing calls briefly at the nest entrance, whereas other birds such as blackbirds don't need any persuasion – they simply start scrambling around the hedgerow surrounding the nest like feathered guerrillas on manoeuvres.

The morning of 30 May had the makings of another glorious day. It was 06.00 as I made my way alongside the river, its level now considerably lower than when the winter storms had made this track impassable only a few months previously. Numerous young rabbits hopped along the track in front of me, still too young to see me as a threat, while further on a young fox cub trotted through a shimmering, hazy blue carpet of bluebells. The world around me felt new, fresh and vibrant.

From the moment I arrived, I could see that the woodpeckers were busy tending to the demands of their brood. As the hours passed that morning, the parents seemed visibly to become ever more tired. They would arrive at the nest individually and perch about a hand's width below the nest, their bills full of food. The chicks would do their utmost to try to reach the food from their wooden ledge without actually letting go. It was incredible to watch how far they were able to stretch out of the hole – their bills would almost reach their parents, but not quite. Sometimes a parent would suddenly shuffle a little bit sideways, as though the chick's sudden subsequent change in direction would allow gravity to lend a hand and then the chick might simply fall out.

But Red was a master at the art of persuasion and his pleading cries always made his parents abandon such seemingly cruel behaviour. They would shuffle a little closer, whereupon he would wrestle the food from their bills and retreat back to perch smugly on the ledge of the nest hole. When either parent bird flew off, it often ventured only a short distance into the canopy, where it sat calling softly *kik… kik… kik* looking back at the nest hole in the hope that one of the chicks would follow. Alas, this was always a forlorn gesture, and after several minutes the parent bird flew off to search for more food before repeating the whole episode again.

I found it interesting that the female seemed to be more determined than her partner when it came to encouraging the chicks to leave. When the male arrived with food he usually flew straight to the nest hole, fed the waiting chick and quickly departed, whereas the female always waited, just out of reach, desperately trying to encourage the chick to take that first faltering step that would take it into its arboreal world.

On this particular morning, the male was feeding, almost without cessation, from the peanut feeders in a local garden. He seemed to be completely focused on going back and forth as fast as possible with as much high-protein food as he could cram into his bill. A round trip, from nest hole to feeders and back to nest hole, was taking him approximately ten minutes. Given that the feeders were four hundred metres from the nest hole 'as the crow flies', he was, for all practical purposes, flying around 6km every hour just to keep his two chicks fed. Is it any wonder he didn't hang around at the nest hole – this was a serious case of a man with a job to do. Perhaps the very fact that he was able to source such a seemingly endless food supply meant that the female was not under as much pressure herself to forage, and could therefore dedicate her time to reassuring the youngsters that it was safe to come out.

Watching the male that morning utilising the peanut feeders brought to mind the often-asked question: should people feed birds in the spring and summer? There was always a fear that by supplying 'easy food', birds would not provide their chicks with sufficient protein, etc. for growth and development.

I admit that watching the woodpeckers going over to the peanut feeders on a daily basis certainly reminded me of parents running down to the local chipper to 'get the tea for the kids' rather than cook a more wholesome meal. However, I think the woodpecker's decision to utilise this food source was not borne out of laziness, of 'not wanting to cook tonight', but rather because woodpeckers are simply programmed to take advantage of certain feeding circumstances.

Over the weeks that I had watched the nest, I had seen them optimize certain food opportunities, from days when both parents fed exclusively in the bracken when click beetles were hatching, to days that they fed endlessly on the woodland floor, chasing ground beetles. Peanuts are a high-protein food, and research has shown that they probably do no harm to developing young birds if fed from dedicated peanut feeders. If they are provided loose on the ground or on a bird table it is a different story, however, and there are many well-documented cases of young birds, especially blue and great tits, which choked to death on whole peanuts. Certainly Red and Black seemed to thrive on this mixed diet of peanuts and insects.

It was now 10.00 and the sun was beating down, the chicks seemingly no closer to leaving now than when I had arrived, four hours earlier, at 06.00. Black was only coming up to the hole about once or twice in every hour, whereas Red quite simply dominated the entrance: he looked like a multi-coloured fluffy tennis ball wedged into it. About two-thirds of Red's body was outside the hole at this point; only his tail and wingtips were not visible as I stared endlessly through the binoculars, praying I wouldn't miss the inevitable. The male arrived shortly after 10.00 and this time he didn't just feed and depart. In a similar manner to the female he 'presented' the food, but from a distance of several centimetres away – close enough that Red could almost touch it, but not quite.

There was a great feeling of excitement and tension in the air at that moment. The whole family was gathered there together as they prepared for this pivotal moment. The male perched silently below the nest hole, pressed tight against the rough bark of the spanish chestnut, with his head craned around and his bill packed with peanuts. Red, now almost hysterical with excitement and indignation, was screaming a crescendo of *Kik* calls as he desperately sought in vain to reach the food. The female, perched nearby on a branch, uttered calls of encouragement. Even Black, sitting in the darkness of the nest chamber, was heard to utter a few calls. Red was throwing his body from side to side as he strained his body forward while clinging desperately to the nest hole.

I watched quietly from my cramped viewpoint, convinced that this was the moment… but just as it seemed that Red had passed the fulcrum point, the male yielded to his offspring's demands and shuffled a few centimetres closer. In a split second, Red had wrestled the peanuts from his father's bill and retreated to his ledge, where he sat smugly looking at his parents.

The male set off once more on his peanut circuit while the female flew quietly into the canopy and silence, of a sort, descended upon the glade. Red was now resting his bill on his upper breast, his eyes starting to close – rather than thinking of leaving the nest, it seemed he was going for a nap. Moments later, the female landed below the nest hole carrying a chafer grub. As before, Red stretched forward as far as he could – and then kept stretching as he scuttled across the bark towards his mother: Red was out!

Because he was effectively going headfirst down a vertical tree trunk, Red spread his incompletely grown wings and stumpy tail out to try and provide extra stability. In doing so, he looked bizarrely like a scruffy mini pterodactyl with his neck stretched out as he clawed his way to his mother. He quickly devoured the chafer grub; probably without even realising he had left the nest. However, now a second problem arose – quite simply, the world was the wrong way around. Trying to rectify the situation and join his mother in the same orientation, Red started to shuffle sideways, looked upwards and then promptly let go and fell off the tree.

Scientists and wildlife filmmakers often recount of being in situations where they witness behaviour and have to restrain themselves from intervening, such as when they see young zebras being attacked by hyenas or great black-backed gulls killing puffins. Often, the hardest part of watching the natural world around us is to do so in an impartial manner, without interfering and without impressing our own morals on the natural events unfolding in front of us. As I watched Red tumbling to the ground, his stumpy wings flapping frantically, I was acutely aware that I was no scientist or wildlife film maker.

I quickly took off my binoculars and squeezed out of the hide, sending the female woodpecker into a frenzy of indignant calling *KIK... KIK... KIK... KIK*. As I hurried across to the tree, I found myself thinking about the barnacle geese in Greenland. These birds nest on cliffs several hundred metres above the glacial valley floors. After the goslings hatch, they have to freefall off the cliff face and bounce their way several hundred metres to the Arctic valley floor, where many are then hoovered up by Arctic foxes, in a manner similar to an aardvark eating ants. Well, no one was going to hoover up Red if I could help it!

When I arrived at the spanish chestnut there was no sign of him, and I realised in my haste to get out that I hadn't actually seen him hit the ground... so where was he? My mind was racing and I could only think of the fox I had seen earlier that morning as I drove along the river.

The female was still calling frantically in the beech tree to my left when I heard a softer, more uncertain, *kik* from a holly bush not too far to my right – and there was Red. A little tousled and with a bit of a blank shell-shocked expression on his face, but otherwise seemingly unharmed. Whether he managed to figure out what the purpose of his wings was before actually hitting the ground or whether he landed and then somehow took off again I'll never know, but at least he was safe.

With a frantic mother calling in the trees above me and Red still trying to figure out how to navigate his way through his new arboreal domain, things were now starting to seem a bit chaotic. The male was due back any minute and Black was still waiting to be fed as well, so I decided against returning to the hide and instead moved about a hundred metres further back from the spanish chestnut tree. I wouldn't be able to follow Red's early adventures any further, but I wanted the family to get settled before I returned to the hide. Sitting under my familiar holly bush, out of view from all but foraging blackbirds and robins, the female's calls began to abate and all I could hear were those of Red as he seemed to move away from the holly bush into the higher reaches of the canopy. A more distant sounding *kik* announced the male's imminent return as he came back from the garden across the river. It always amazed me how far carrying his contact calls were, especially with a bill full of peanuts. I waited a further ten minutes until the woodland seemed a lot quieter, and, with neither of the parents sounding alarm calls, I quickly and discreetly made my way back into the hide.

With Red, the stronger of the two, now fledged, Black had the nest hole to himself, as well as the seemingly undivided attention of his father. It is a strange characteristic of great spotted woodpeckers that while the parents share the feeding duties when their young are in the nest, once the chicks have fledged they often divide their offspring amongst them, each adult bird caring for one or two youngsters. In this case, it seemed that the female was going to be responsible for Red, since I never saw her return to the tree for the rest of that day, leaving the male alone with the task.

I was keen to assess what stage of development Black had reached. In the past few days he had featured very little at the entrance hole, and based on what I'd seen he certainly hadn't received as much food as his sibling, who had spent the last few days commandeering the nest hole. With Red now fledged, a strange silence had descended on the clearing, the continuous, almost endless *kik... kik... kik... kik... kik... kik* he had maintained had now ceased and Black, by contrast, was surprisingly silent.

As I watched the tree from the hide, I could hear Red further up the woodland. The calls of juvenile woodpeckers are generally considered to be identical to those of the adults; however, for the first few days after they have left the nest, I can usually pick out a difference. The young birds seem to lack the stridency and clarity of the adults and have a slightly softer and mellower tone. In many ways it is as though they yet lack the confidence to 'let rip' and pierce the woodland with the ice-clear sharpness of the adults, but given time they will.

It was now well after midday and I knew I would shortly have to leave. Having watched one youngster take to the wing I was keen also to see the second fledge. However, with woodpeckers, fledging is an agonizingly drawn out process and I knew that the second bird could well have remained in the nest all the following day.

A few moments later the male arrived silently on the tree. Through my binoculars I could clearly see the pinkish-brown and white colouring of peanuts in his bill; he was still availing of the peanut feeders in the garden on the far side of the river. Black, on hearing his father's approach, had come up to the entrance hole and was calling for food. This was the first time in a few days I had seen him properly, and once again I was surprised at how little red plumage was on his crown; a small garnet topknot, so different from his sibling's blaze of crimson. Black's character was also markedly different: he showed none of Red's noisy boisterousness or self-assuredness, but rather a surprising meekness and almost shyness. He was not nearly as vocal as Red and had a far less voracious appetite. Once fed, he usually retreated quietly into the chamber, rather than sitting on the ledge and calling incessantly in the same manner as Red. In our society we would probably have referred to him as 'a quiet child' or 'the withdrawn type'.

I was curious as to whether this was due to his character or whether something was amiss. Was he the weaker of the two, still struggling to survive, or was he just an unobtrusive fledgling? The interval between the male's visits increased, until by early afternoon he was returning about every twenty-five or thirty minutes. Since I knew that a return trip to the feeders took only about ten minutes, I suspected that he was also making trips to feed Red or perhaps was simply foraging for himself. As I left the woodland and made my way back along the track, I saw the female foraging on a decaying birch on the slope below me. With minimal effort she extracted a large white grub from the crumbling timber and flew back up the slope into the canopy, where no doubt Red was eagerly awaiting her return.

I returned later that day shortly after 16.00. It was a hot afternoon, making me glad of the shelter under the shade of the now full woodland canopy. I had just begun walking up the slope when an agitated *Kik* from the nearby trees announced my arrival. Birds were still in the area, at any rate, but was Black still in the nest? I slid into the hide as quietly as I could, noting another *Kik*, this time from further up the slope. It was a calm afternoon and the midges were tenacious and unrelenting outside; although I was protected from much of the assault by being in the hide, I knew that it was only a matter of time before they worked their way inside.

As I sat and watched, I was aware that there was no sound coming from the nest. This didn't greatly concern me, however, as youngsters often doze between feeds and Black was the quieter of the two siblings. From time to time I heard an occasional *Kik* in various parts of the canopy, but in all cases the calls were very adult-sounding, presumably made by one of the adults foraging. Finally after almost three quarters of an hour had passed, the male alighted alongside the nest hole carrying food. He perched there in profile without a sound, motionless, and the nest hole responded with an equal absence of noise. Finally, there was movement and Black reached his head out to be fed. I had hoped that he would still be there, affording me the opportunity to see the conclusion of the story, as it were... but the sight of him being fed didn't bring the joy I had expected.

His movements seemed sluggish and his silence was surprising after those weeks of 'purring' 'piping' and 'kikking'. I couldn't put my finger on it, but he certainly didn't seem like a bird about to fly. Was I imagining it or being over analytical? There was no single aspect of his behaviour that indicated anything was amiss yet my gut instinct was concern.

Having fed his solitary charge, the male hopped up onto his favourite spur and began preening, his long tongue writhing around his feathers like the fall of a whip. As he went about his business, Black started to call at the entrance hole *kik... kik*. Not particularly strong-sounding, but still loud enough to give me hope that all was indeed well. The male, finished his preening, flew off with a single *Kik* and disappeared towards the river. Unlike the numerous times I had witnessed him feeding Red in the preceding twenty-four hours, he didn't seem to have any inclination towards encouraging Black to leave the nest, either by coaxing him with food or encouraging him with calls.

Black had stopped calling by now and was looking around the woodland, first at the surrounding tree trunks, then downwards at the woodland floor and finally upwards towards the canopy, the place he needed to reach. As I watched him through my binoculars, he blinked a couple of times and then disappeared from view, into the tree.

Little was I to know that I would never see him alive again.

After a further twenty minutes, the male again alighted on the tree with a bill full of food; the female was seemingly devoting her time to Red's wellbeing. He waited for a few seconds, and when no chick appeared he hopped his way up to the nest hole entrance and waited again: still no response. He called, and when he once again received no answer he flew off, still carrying the food. Ten minutes later he returned briefly, and with no reply he flew off again.

By now the midges had well and truly found me. Sitting in the almost airless stillness of my hide, I was sweating heavily and being bitten all over, as hundreds of 'no-see-ums' fought over my skin. The paper in my notebook was sticking together where my wet fingers, hands and arms touched the pages. A further half hour passed before the male returned with food once more. This time, when he received no response, he went inside the nest hole, wiggling his tail feathers as he disappeared from view. When he emerged a few seconds later I was surprised to see that he still had food in his bill. He sat alongside the nest hole, seemingly unsure as to what he should do next. He poked his head back into the nest hole a few times, but each time the food remained firmly in his mouth. He could obviously see Black but was getting no response – was he asleep? Finally, almost as though he couldn't think of anything else to do, he ate the food himself. He spent a further two or three minutes quietly pecking at the sides of the hole entrance in the same aimless manner as I had seen him doing earlier in the season; it was almost like he was trying to figure out what to do from now on. After one further quick look into the hole, he flew back up to the canopy.

Fifteen minutes later he was back – but this time he wasn't carrying food, and in the time he had been gone there had been no sign of activity from within the nest. He was perched below the hole and, as he started making his way up the tree, he hopped past the entrance, hesitated momentarily, and then hopped on up to the top of the tree, where he paused for a short preen before flying off.

After that, I never saw him return to the tree again. As the evening began to close in, the question remained unanswered – was Black alive? I made my way down the slope and along the river while tossing this question, and others, around in my head, when my thoughts were disturbed by a quiet *Kik*. It wasn't the harsh alarm or contact call of an adult, but the softer note of a youngster. I looked up and saw Red feeding quietly by himself on a lichen-covered branch of a small birch alongside the river. Feeding was probably a bit of a misnomer, since young woodpeckers are still fed by their parents for a couple of weeks after leaving the nest and Red wasn't even out of the nest a full day. Still, instinct would guide him as to how best to survive in this new world he was encountering and he seemed to be making a good start as he sat on the branch, pecking half-heartedly at the flaking bark. He was quite unperturbed by my presence and hopped slowly along the branch giving an occasional quiet, contented *Kik*. There was no sign of either parent in attendance, which I thought was surprising, as he seemed quite vulnerable and exposed on the branch. Alone and innocent of the dangers of the world around him, he could make an easy snack for a passing sparrowhawk; one of the main threats to young woodpeckers.

When I returned to the wood early the following morning I immediately knew – it was over. There is a certain air of silence that tells you that the nest site is now deserted, a certainty that only comes with experience. Other birds were still calling and feeding, of course, and thrushes, tits and finches were still present in abundance, but the family I had spent so much time with had gone. The absence of any woodpecker calls or pecking sounds after so many weeks of activity made this woodland a quieter place, and although they had left with success, I was saddened that my routine on the banks of the Avonmore River was now drawing to a close.

I made my way up to the spanish chestnut tree and decided to go into the hide for an hour or so, just in case birds were still in the area, but the deafening silence remained throughout. As I prepared to leave, I went over to the tree itself and noticed two feathers on the ground directly beneath the entrance hole. Surprisingly, they were two tail feathers from a young woodpecker. Woodpecker tail feathers are readily identifiable by their long pointed tips and black and white markings. The bases of the feathers were still in their quill sheaths, indicating they were from a still incompletely-feathered young bird. It was interesting to feel how stiff the feathers were, even at this stage; so different from the soft feathers normally associated with birds. These feathers were rigid and built to take abuse, as they steadied the bird during its arboreal carpentry. But where had they come from? One possible explanation was that Black had tried to fly last night at dusk and fallen to the ground, only to be predated by a passing fox or pine marten. Had it been earlier in the season, they could have come from a chick which, having died in the nest, was subsequently thrown out by the parents. Alternatively, when Red fell off the tree after leaving the nest, perhaps his frantic struggling had dislodged the feathers. I placed them in my pocket as a memento of the season and headed home. My work here was done.

Great spotted woodpeckers never remain in the immediate natal area very long after leaving the nest and tend to range quite widely, either as a single group or divided into two parties, each with one parent. They don't return to the nest at any stage, and it is uncertain as to whether they roost together as a family or simply forage together during the day before roosting individually, dispersed throughout the surrounding woodlands.

From previous years' experience, I knew that the adults usually brought the young birds to the peanut feeders in the garden on the far side of the river. I called into the homeowners and told them that at least one bird had fledged from the nest and that there was uncertainty about the fate of the second, and I asked them to let me know if and when they appeared.

Over the years that the woodpeckers had used this garden, they always followed a predictable routine after fledging. The adults would carry on visiting the feeders, but they wouldn't bring the youngsters into the garden for up to a week after fledging. Instead, they would take the food out of the garden to whatever part of the surrounding countryside in which their young were hiding. After several days the adults would change their behaviour: instead of flying straight out of the garden, they would instead fly up to the canopy of the tallest trees along the garden boundary where the young were hidden from view, but identifiable by the fact the adult quickly returned to the feeder with a now empty bill.

Gradually the youngsters would get stronger and more confident, and after another day or two would join their parents on the peanut feeder, either being fed by mum and dad alongside them or enthusiastically hammering away themselves at the peanuts.

Several days after I had visited the house, I received the expected phone call. Amazingly, the adults were feeding not one but two youngsters on the feeders – Black had made it. What had been going on during those closing hours at the nest I will never quite figure out, but the fact he had made it, along with his sibling, was fantastic news. It appeared to be shaping up to be another successful year for the 'Spanish Chestnut Woodpeckers'.

A few days later I received another call from the residents of the house to say they had something to show me. I arrived with great expectations – had a third youngster somehow appeared? Instead, I was handed a small plastic bag. Inside lay the little body of a woodpecker – it was Black.

The world outside the safety of the nest is a dangerous one and there is so much natural wastage with every species, just to keep a population on an even keel, that I shouldn't have been surprised, let alone upset, by this development. But this wasn't just a statistic or a calculated loss; this was Black, a friend and a familiar face I had watched for weeks and whose feathered visage I knew intimately. No, this wasn't a statistic: this was a tragedy.

The circumstances of his death were straightforward enough. Feeding on the peanut feeder, he had taken off and, mistaking the reflection of the trees and sky in a nearby window for his home woodland, he had flown into the glass, killing himself instantly. There is no doubting that he was the weaker of the two, for whatever reason, and survival of the fittest dictated his days were numbered. Perhaps his wings were not strong enough to clear the window, or perhaps his reactions were not yet quick enough to save him when he realised the tree he was heading for had changed into something less welcoming.

Unfortunately, it is quite common for birds to strike glass windows, and this was not the first time I had been handed a young woodpecker in a bag. A few years previously, several kilometres away, two woodpeckers had been killed by collisions with windows in a garden

Red was out!

they were visiting; both were also youngsters. Many households across Ireland feed birds throughout the year, and especially during winter months. There is no doubt that doing so helps many more thousands of birds survive than would otherwise do so, especially with the ever-increasing pace of habitat loss. However, feeding birds artificially has always brought risks. Concentrating birds into one small dining area makes it easier for their natural predators, such as sparrowhawks, to make a kill. Attracting birds into our human-altered environment also exposes them to unnatural predators, particularly the domestic cat, as well as exposing them to man-made threats, as in this case.

I took Black's body home and gently placed him in the freezer. His part in the story was finished, but perhaps he would be of some use to researchers involved in biometrics, DNA and other aspects of ornithology, far removed from my own fields of expertise.

With only one juvenile now to care for, the parents would not be under as much pressure as before and they could now both devote all their efforts into caring for him. Certainly, the few sightings of Red I had made whilst at the house had revealed him to be in good health and seemingly strong.

A week later, I received another phone call...

This time it was Red that lay at the bottom of the plastic bag. I stared at the pathetic feathered bundle in disbelief. Only a matter of weeks had passed since that morning he had first scrambled across the bark of the spanish chestnut, his senses being blown open by the magical new world he must surely have felt he had become part of... and now he was dead.

The circumstances of Red's death differed from those of Black's. He was found in the middle of the garden, away from the feeders and nearby windows which had claimed the life of his sibling, and was lying under a bush. A cursory glance showed he had been predated, as much of his back had been eaten away, yet he had not been plucked in the usual manner that a sparrowhawk would employ when eating its prey. A sparrowhawk was the most likely predator, however, as they are agile hunters and adept at pursuing birds through trees and shrubbery, catching their prey on the wing. Great spotted woodpeckers form a regular part of their diet in other European countries.

Another possibility was that Red had in fact hit the window after all, killing himself, and was found by a predator which took the body off to the shrubbery only to be disturbed before it had finished feeding: a pine marten or stoat would be the most likely suspect in this scenario. Either way, there was no changing the game result: 'woodpeckers 0'

I gently laid Red's body in the freezer alongside that of his sibling. Written on the bags containing their bodies were their names and the dates on which they had died. Also in the same compartment was an adult female great spotted woodpecker, found freshly killed by a pine marten the previous summer at a nest site several kilometres away. In time, each of these birds was sent to Trinity College, Dublin for research purposes, with some even ending up on public display as mounted specimens.

I was in a sombre mood that evening; the story had finished abruptly in a manner so unexpected that it had left me empty. So much had been learnt over the previous few months and so many exciting events had unfolded right in front of my eyes, and yet one stark fact remained uppermost in my mind...

The spanish chestnut siblings were dead.

6.
WOODLAND INHABITANTS

SPENDING TIME ALONE in the woods, often just sitting still for hours on end, may seem strange, if not just plain odd, to those not accustomed to it. Some people relish solitude whilst others crave activity; I am fortunate in that I enjoy both. While watching woodpeckers may sound like an exciting activity, the reality is that a lot of time is actually spent not watching woodpeckers, but that doesn't mean that there's nothing to see.

All mammals rely on their senses to navigate the world around them. By sitting very still in a hide you eliminate the risk of being discovered by the sharp eyes and super-sensitive ears with which many of the woodpecker's neighbours are graced. While it is very hard to mask the scent of a human from the keen nose of a passing mammal, I have rarely found this to be a problem. Many of our native animals are accustomed to the scent of people and while they may be wary of it, they won't avoid a place just because a person recently passed by. Furthermore, while some birds have a sense of smell, they seem to use it for finding specific foods rather than locating potential predators. Sitting in the hide, or even hidden under my nearby holly bush, provided me with numerous opportunities to watch some of the other wildlife that shared the world my woodpeckers lived in and to see how they possibly even affected their lives.

Sika deer were frequent visitors to the woodland glade surrounding the spanish chestnut tree. Graceful and coy, they would step out of the densely shaded undergrowth into the dappled sunlight of the glade. So quiet was their approach that I often suddenly became aware of them standing in front of me with no idea whence they had materialised. They would stand there, with one leg raised in suspense, as though holding their breaths, waiting for a sound such as a breaking twig, which would send them bounding back into the undergrowth on stiff rigid legs, almost as though they were on springs. Beautiful as they were, often standing only twenty metres in front of me with the dappled green tinted sunlight dancing over the russet coats, I had sadly to remind myself that they did not belong here in this woodland – their home was over 8,000 kilometres away.

Sika Deer are native to north-eastern Asia. Four individuals, one stag and three hinds, were introduced in 1860 to Powerscourt Estate, County Wicklow. Descendants of just these four individuals subsequently escaped and gave rise to the current population. Estimates vary as to the number of sikas in County Wicklow. The 13,000 animals which are culled by the National Parks and Wildlife Service each year quite likely only represent a small percentage of the total Wicklow population. They are a classic example of the environmental problems mankind's interference can create. The glade where my woodpeckers were nesting had little ground cover and there were no seedling trees growing since the young fresh growth in spring is much appreciated by the deer following the hardship of winter. The woodpeckers' spanish chestnut tree had stood here for around a hundred years, perhaps more, yet for all that time none of its offspring had got a foothold in this glade to replace it when eventually it falls. The daily grazing of sika deer during the intervening decades was certainly a contributing factor, in my opinion.

It was interesting to see the woodpeckers going about their business of raising a family alongside the sikas. Both species are comparatively recent additions to Ireland's fauna, yet each has a radically different story of how it has come to occupy the same glade. In some ways, the woodpeckers benefitted from the deer's presence, for I often saw them foraging on the open ground, bounding along through the leaf litter. If the deer were not grazing here, then this glade would quite likely be covered in bilberry bushes and would provide ideal cover for predators to lie in wait for an unsuspecting woodpecker.

The fact that sika deer are not native to this country did not detract from their delicate beauty in any way. It is not through any fault of their own, other than being adaptive and opportunistic, that they are considered pests. Not a day would pass when I was watching the woodpeckers that I would not be joined by parties of deer. Usually it was small groups of nervous and jittery hinds, but occasionally a stag would accompany them, flicking his ears back and forth as he maintained a constant vigil, even as he grazed. Fawns, or calves, as they are more correctly called, never featured in these daily visits and would not appear until they had been born in mid-June.

The woodpeckers had other regular visitors as well and surprisingly one of these was the Irish hare. Hares are not animals that one normally associates with woodlands; usually they prefer flat, open landscapes such as arable fields, saltmarshes and open moors. Whenever they appeared in the woodland they always looked most ungainly as they hopped slowly along, grazing the sparse vegetation. A hare is an athlete and, as such, is built for speed and endurance, with long muscular legs to propel itself across its preferred open terrain. But here, amongst the trees and tangled undergrowth, there was no room for the elegance of speed, and the long hind legs looked ungainly and unwieldly. The presence of hares in the wood surprised me, because during the countless hours I watched the woodpeckers, not once did I see a rabbit. Possibly the hares were not actually residing in the wood but moved through it from one feeding area to another. Even so, it was a risky business as they would not have been able to run from a fox as quickly as if they had been on the open hillsides.

Not all of the woodland inhabitants were as benign towards the woodpeckers as the deer and hare, and nor were they as easy to watch. Several years previously, another pair of woodpeckers had nested less than a kilometre from the spanish chestnut tree and had successfully raised a family in a nest hole located about ten metres above the ground. When I returned to that nest the following spring, to check if the birds had returned, I was shocked to see that the hole had been destroyed. The whole entrance had been widened and enlarged seemingly by something trying to get in – something considerably bigger than a woodpecker. A close examination of the wood on the outside of the hole revealed claw and scratch marks, and not many mammals with sharp teeth and claws can climb ten metres up a tree.

Of all our native mammals, none has ever captured my imagination since my youth in the manner that the pine marten has. Known as *Cat Crainn*, meaning 'tree cat', in Irish, its pure elusiveness and wildness puts it in a class of its own.

When I was growing up and devouring every new book on wildlife, that I could find, it was an animal that, in Great Britain, was seemingly confined to the Scottish Highlands, where it lived an isolated life with the equally enigmatic Scottish wildcat. Its rarity, rugged beauty and evasiveness enchanted me from an early age and continues to do so today. Although widespread in Ireland until the late nineteenth century, it was hunted and persecuted until, by the early twentieth century, it was absent from much of its former range. By the 1980s it had been reduced to isolated pockets in Clare, Donegal and Fermanagh. I found it interesting that the pine marten formerly occurred throughout many of the woodlands that the great spotted woodpecker subsequently colonised.

To see my first pine martens I had to travel to Scotland, where by spending long nights sleeping in cars in various parks I was finally able to see them rummaging through the dustbins of several National Trust properties by moonlight, with the majestic Cairngorm Mountains looming darkly in the background; a magical experience. Even just twenty years ago, finding them in Ireland was still far from easy, and when I finally watched a half-grown kit feeding in a woodland in County Fermanagh, I had spent two full days and nights living in a small hide designed for the purpose. Sometimes watching wildlife behaving naturally in its true environment requires arduous perseverance – but always it is worth it, not just for the views and fortunate insights but often for the experience in itself.

By the late twentieth century, circumstances changed for Ireland's pine martens, and the species slowly began expanding its range eastwards once more, finally crossing the Shannon in the early 2000s. When exactly it arrived back in Wicklow is a topic of debate. Certainly when I found the woodpeckers' nest hole that had been attacked, breeding had yet to be confirmed in County Wicklow. There had, in fact, only been one confirmed live sighting, as well as a road casualty on the Wicklow Gap.

The fact that they were now living in the same woodland as the great spotted woodpecker interested me for many reasons. Both were new arrivals to this woodland, one colonising from the east and one recapturing old territory from the west: a predator and its prey meeting for the first time, as in Ireland their paths had never crossed before. More importantly, they were the only predator I knew that posed a risk to the young in the nest because pine martens, although primarily terrestrial, have no problem climbing ten or fifteen metres up a tree. In other countries, great spotted woodpecker nests must endure other tree climbing threats, such as weasels and snakes. When they first colonised Wicklow, their nests faced few dangers, but perhaps this is now set to change and their range expansion may start slowing.

Although watching woodpeckers was my primary reason for being in this woodland, the opportunity potentially to watch pine martens to boot was like being given ice cream and asked if you wanted jelly to go with it! Compared to woodpeckers, pine martens are a head-

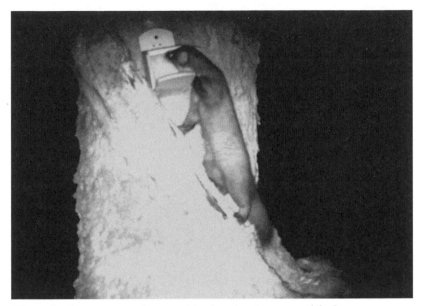

The male pine marten only ever visited under the cover of darkness

wrecking species to observe in any manner other than random chance sightings. One Irish wildlife author wrote several chapters on their lifestyle without ever seeing one, while a researcher monitored several families for years in dense woodland but never saw them, other than by live trapping. Solving the Rubik's Cube was a more attainable goal it seemed.

Woodpeckers were active during the day, quite vocal and brightly marked and although thinly distributed they had small territories. pine martens were the direct opposite: mostly nocturnal, almost completely silent, the same colour as parts of the woodland itself and usually solitary hunters across large territories measuring several square kilometres. The individual which had attacked the nest hole in this woodland could have travelled from any of the surrounding woodlands several kilometres in any direction, or could simply have been a wandering male passing through without any thought of returning. However, once I started watching the pair of woodpeckers at the spanish chestnut tree I knew I wanted to find out more about this particular threat to them.

Mammal-watching is very different from birdwatching: it is usually a lot more challenging and therefore, in many ways, more rewarding. I have been observing mammals and their behaviour in their natural habitats since I was a young teenager. Naturally some mammals are easier to see than others; for example rabbits are simple compared to badgers but a badger is considerably easier than an otter. I have spent many nights over the years sitting in bare wind-swept trees, crouched uncomfortably under wet gorse bushes and walking across frozen landscapes thick with snow and lit by nothing other than an unimaginably cold moon watching foxes, badgers and even otters; but these had something that a pine marten rarely has – routine. In simple terms, most mammals have a home to which they are tied for a considerable part of their lives, and once you locate the rabbit warren, badger sett or fox's 'lie up'[10] then the task of observation becomes so much easier. However, from studies carried out by radio tracking, it is known that pine martens rarely spend the day lying up in the same spot, rarely have their kits in the same den in subsequent years and often spend each day in a different part of their territory. To be honest, the same can be said about many species of birds we see every day in our gardens, but because there are so many more birds we rarely notice their individual habits.

Like the birds we feed in our gardens and in the same manner as woodpeckers are attracted to peanut feeders, mammals can be lured into showing themselves by leaving out food for them, especially if it's a food that they find irresistible. Badgers love peanut butter and chocolate-covered raisins, hedgehogs love eggs – and pine martens love strawberry jam!

As I sat in the hide during the days when the woodpeckers were incubating their eggs, I tried to come up with a way to record pine martens in the area. Simply putting out bait on an afternoon would achieve nothing; a fox going about his nocturnal wanderings would

---

[10] Unlike badgers and rabbits, foxes only live underground for a few months in the spring while rearing their cubs. During the rest of the year, they sleep above ground in a sheltered spot, such as under an overhanging bank or in dense undergrowth.

The Huntress of the Land

eat any bait long before a pine marten had even awoken. As I was sitting in the hide one morning, I saw a red squirrel bounding across the glade and I remembered a wooden squirrel feeder I had in my shed. It was a peculiarly designed feeder which I had first seen being used very effectively in Scotland. It consisted of a wooden box with a Perspex window through which the squirrel could see the food; he then had to lift the hinged lid to get at the food inside. A few days later I fitted my squirrel feeder onto a tree in a different part of the woodland. It was about two metres off the ground; above the reach of any curious fox yet low enough that a passing pine marten could easily access it. The hinged lid prevented birds from taking any of the food, and I hoped that the type of bait I was planning to use would deter red squirrels. Although pine martens are primarily carnivorous, they enjoy a varied diet that includes fruit, eggs and insects. However, their weakness is sugar, and where this is on offer they have no more will power than a six-year-old child does in a chocolate factory!

I crammed the feeder with crumbled custard creams, peanuts, chocolate covered raisins, crackers with Nutella and pieces of bread covered in strawberry jam; surely a concoction that no pine marten could resist?

Each day, before I settled into the hide to watch the woodpeckers, I checked the feeder for any signs that might indicate a pine marten's presence; but the food remained untouched and after several days started to go mouldy. Maybe there were no martens in the area and the attack that had been carried out on that nest hole had simply been the work of a passing individual.

After a week had passed, I cleaned out the untouched food, washed out the feeder and refilled it. This time, in addition to the food in the feeder, I also smeared strawberry jam into several of the crevices of the oak tree itself. Once again, several days passed without anything changing, other than increasing numbers of wasps appearing as the scent of the jam lured them in as though to a honey trap... and then the food was gone.

Unlike the woodpeckers whose behaviour was visible daily, if not always understandable, all I had after two weeks of mammal study was a wooden feeder, which after two weeks was emptied between the hours of 16.40 and 09.30 the following day. Not exactly riveting information it has to be said, especially as I could not say for certain even what had removed the food.

I refilled the feeder with yet more calorie-laden goodies and this time I placed a motion-activated camera alongside it. These small cameras, commonly referred to as trail cameras, are a useful asset for wildlife observation since they can 'watch' a specific area while you are away and record either still images or video. They are definitely not foolproof, however, and due to the slight delay between the sensor and the shutter you often end up with blank images. Once again, almost a week had passed without any food being taken, yet the camera recorded an interesting account of what went on in the woodland during my absence. Countless photographs of Sika deer of all ages showed that although they were active throughout the day and night they were at their most active around dawn. A fox showed up one night shortly after midnight showing great interest in the bait, which he was clearly unable to reach as one of the photographs showed him standing on his back legs alongside the tree. After posing for several more photos, he moved on.

Finally the bait was taken and an examination of the camera files showed the culprit – a very large and most likely male pine marten standing upright on his heavily muscled hind legs, his claws visible as he gripped the rough bark of the tree while he stretched his neck and lithe shoulders up towards the feeder. His slender head was completely stuck into the feeder as he satisfied his sugar craving for the night. His tail, almost half his entire body length and undoubtedly the most luscious and impressive of any Irish mammal – surpassing even that of the red squirrel – draped down the tree like that of a snow leopard in the Himalayas. The image that captured this moment was taken at 02.30 using infra-red and unfortunately showed the pine marten only in black and white. His thick pelt showed up as black whereas in daylight it is a rich chocolate brown of a tone that no other Irish mammal or bird portrays. His throat appeared white whereas it is really a gorgeous, rich, creamy yellow interrupted with a few random blobs of chestnut, as though a painter had flicked a brush on it. His ears were also the same rich creamy yellow.

Throughout the months I was in the hide watching the woodpecker, I kept the feeder well stocked but never actually saw the male pine marten. Rather than let him die from diabetes, I changed the bait to a more natural and healthier blend of wholemeal bread, fruit and kitchen scraps; with a little bit of jam as a treat, which he didn't seem to object to. He never became a regular visitor, usually only turning up about once a week. Clearly he was not residing in the area and was ranging over a large territory. From the woodpeckers' point of view this was good news, since their young had now hatched and were becoming more vocal with each passing day, thereby increasing the chances of their being noticed. Shortly before the young flew, the camera recorded a different, slightly smaller pine marten. I felt this was most likely a female, since it was not small enough for a young kit and the larger resident male would not tolerate another intruding male. Once she started to make an appearance he seemed to disappear, as there were no further pictures of him recorded. She was a regular, but not nightly, visitor during late May, and her pattern of arriving at a variety of times from after sunset to anytime during the night suggested that, unlike the male, she was residing in or close to the woodland.

The young woodpeckers had by now flown and so I was no longer in the hide on a daily basis, which meant the woodland was probably quieter with fewer signs of my passing. I stopped by every one to two days to fill the feeder. The female marten was now very active and would often arrive during daylight hours, providing stunning colour poses in a natural woodland setting; her rich chestnut fur gleamed with lustre like old furniture and her creamy throat was such a rich thick yellow it was almost like she was covered in Jersey cream. Every part of her slender frame oozed grace, sinuousness and elegance; she was a true huntress of the land.

My suspicions that she was residing in the woodland were confirmed a few weeks later when a series of nocturnal photographs showed not just her but four kits as well. With so many mouths to feed, no wonder she had been such a frequent visitor over the preceding weeks. It was comical looking at the photographs of four martens all trying to get their heads into the feeder at the same time; it was completely enveloped in dark fur, while four tails, with varying degrees of bushiness, stuck out at right angles like a furry St. Brigid's Cross!

Throughout June and July, the pine marten family of continued to grow and to explore the woodland, and they came to the feeder continuously. There was no pattern to their comings and goings, and they could just as easily arrive during mid-morning or early afternoon as during the darkest hours of the night. They did their own thing and as a result were impossible to predict; it was no surprise then that, try as I might, I could not catch a glimpse of them. I sat in the hide, I sat under the holly tree and I sat in the car – but it made no difference, they were just too elusive. Frustratingly, one series of photographs showed me filling the feeder and two pine martens feeding on it less than ten minutes later. Had they been watching me?

One hot sultry evening in mid-July as I arrived in the woodland I heard a blackbird giving its *chink... chink... chink* alarm call from a steep bank ahead of me that was covered in bilberry bushes. As I approached the bank something small, dark and fast shot along the bank into thicker vegetation. It was so fast that I could see no detail on it and its elusiveness, wariness and speed meant it wouldn't be returning while I was there.

That fleeting glimpse of a pine marten is often all that people see of this woodland hunter, and in that I was no different. Yet, I felt no disappointment as the ample insights I had gained through my recordings at the feeder made me feel that I had really come to know this family, even though I never saw them directly. My observations proved that pine martens had returned and were breeding in County Wicklow again for the first time since the species had been exterminated there at the beginning of the twentieth century. Furthermore, they were most likely the first photographs taken of pine martens in their natural habitat in County Wicklow, since the species had been absent for many decades. This goes to show that the contributions of casual observers are often of great value when it comes to building up the overall picture of a species.

There were never any indications that year that the pine martens expressed any interest in, or even awareness of, the woodpeckers' nest close by. This is quite intriguing, especially given that during the final week before they leave the nest the young woodpeckers can easily be heard a hundred metres away and the spanish chestnut tree, with its broken spurs and chiselled bark, was easily climbed. So were pine martens actually a threat to great spotted woodpeckers? Although the woodpeckers in this woodland were left unbothered, other pairs in County Wicklow were not so lucky.

Several kilometres away another pair of woodpeckers had a nest on the steep slopes of one of the glaciated valleys. It was a mature oakwood with a dense understory of bracken, bramble and scrub. The woodpeckers had nested in a dead oak tree thickly covered with ivy and the young had hatched considerably later than the young in the spanish chestnut tree. Because of this I was able to watch this pair, and other late-hatching pairs, for several weeks after the others had left the nest. My casual observations were made without the use of the hide and often took the form of checking what nests still had chicks in them while walking my dalmatian in the evening. One evening in late June I arrived and found the nest unexpectedly silent, which was surprising since the young were not expected to fly for several days yet and had been extremely vocal on previous evenings. I waited for a short while, but my dalmatian, as usual, was full of restless energy – so remaining still and hidden was not an option. As we headed down the slope, she suddenly took off into the bracken after something which ran ahead of her, its presence given away by a Mexican wave effect through the swaying fronds, subsequently being flattened by a bounding spotted frame. I assumed it was a rabbit and as I followed on down the slope, suddenly and unexpectedly, there at my feet lay a dead female great spotted woodpecker.

Although I had been watching woodpeckers daily for months, the unexpected sight of one lying in front of me took me by surprise. It lay there, as though asleep, with not a feather out of place. There were no marks, blood or any signs of predation on its small, feathered body. I gently lifted it up and cradled it in my hand; it was still warm and the feathers on its breast had small droplets of water from the damp grass where it had been dropped. It was so perfect that I almost expected it to open its eyes and struggle to escape my grip; it simply lacked the breath of life, its *scintillula*.[11] As I looked down on it, waiting for my spotted companion to return from her fruitless chase, the rank smell of musk rose from its pied plumage; the scent of a pine marten.

How the woodpecker came to be killed is a mystery. Most likely, she was feeding on the ground, hunting amongst the bracken for click beetles as I had seen other woodpeckers do when feeding young, and

---

[11]   Scintillula: The small spark of the soul

was pounced on by the pine marten. But I had been in and around the nest for almost a quarter of an hour and the corpse had showed no signs of being eaten. Perhaps the marten had not caught it at the nest site but elsewhere and simply happened to have passed by the nest tree on her way to feed her kits? An intriguing possibility is that she might have been attracted to the nest by the noise of the hungry youngsters and had hidden amongst the ivy surrounding the nest hole, lying in wait for the unsuspecting female to return to the nest. Whether the young birds subsequently starved and died or were taken by the pine marten I never discovered, but there was no more activity seen at that nest.

This wasn't the only confirmed casualty of the increasing pine marten population in Wicklow. A number of nest holes across the county were now showing signs of being attacked and enlarged, and in one case, in coniferous woodland seven kilometres away, a family of woodpeckers was taken by a pine marten breaking into the nest from the back of the tree. All the young were predated in a single attack. Reports by observers in other counties told of nests being attacked, primarily by enlarging the nest hole itself.

Although the great spotted woodpecker has now become a new addition to the Irish pine martens' diet, they are not responsible in any way for the increase in the numbers of pine martens in Wicklow. The pine marten had been expanding its range eastwards long before the woodpeckers first began to colonise Ireland as a breeding species. It is interesting to consider the possibility that the lack of a mammalian predator at the time of their arrival may have been a factor that enabled them to form a beachhead before beginning to expand further. It is natural, from an emotional human point of view, to consider the native pine marten as the 'bad guy' in the interaction of these two species. However, nature is better at sorting the balance than mankind has ever been and we should refrain from interfering with the natural biodiversity of the world based on how we feel it should function. Playing God never improves things; the original plan was laid down long before mankind took its first tentative steps out of Africa. An example of the dangers of playing God can be found in many parts of

Ireland, though thankfully the creature in question was absent from the woods where I roamed, namely, the grey squirrel. Introduced in 1911 from North America to a private estate in County Longford, it quickly spread to many parts of Ireland, displacing the native red squirrel in the process and raising the possibility of its potential extinction.

In the early 2000s grey squirrels were present in County Wicklow, close to where I lived. However, they have now gone and red squirrels are doing quite well once again and are increasing in numbers. This is partly due to the corresponding increase in pine martens. Red squirrels are considerably lighter and more nimble than their grey cousins and they are able to travel on lighter, smaller branches high in the canopies; branches which are unable to support the weight of either pine marten or grey squirrel. Furthermore, they spend less time on the ground compared to grey squirrels, leaving them less vulnerable to ground predation. The larger and heavier grey squirrel is far more likely to be taken by pine martens and this seems to have been the reason for their demise.

Red squirrels are the epitome of cuteness and it is no wonder you can buy a cuddly red squirrel in a toy shop more readily than a cuddly pine marten. A pair of red squirrels were daily visitors to the glade where I had erected my hide, providing light relief through the long hours with their nimble acrobatic activities. Although they sometimes take birds' eggs, they never seemed to interfere with the woodpeckers; perhaps because the woodpeckers were almost the same size and possessed a serious weapon, namely their chisel-like bill.

The speed at which a red squirrel can move through the trees is breathtakingly beautiful to watch. They seem to be able to assess in a split second whether or not the thinnest twigs imaginable will support their lithe bodies as they leap from tree to tree. They are truly the embodiment of the woodland will-o'-the-wisp as they pass overhead in a haze of russet-toned fur. Unlike many other Irish mammals, they are far from silent and often chitter noisily as they chase each other in ever decreasing spiralling trails up the lichen-covered trees, sending showers of green speckled rain tumbling to the woodland floor.

One morning in early April, my arrival was greeted by a loud scratching sound from a nearby oak. Looking up I saw two red squirrels facing each other, one clinging to the trunk of the tree facing upwards while the other mirrored his position exactly as though he were a reflection. They stamped their feet excitedly as the lower individual tried to get past, their tiny claws scraping bits of bark and lichen off the tree like handfuls of confetti as they chittered and squeaked at each other before chasing each other all the way down to the woodland floor. Each was totally engrossed in the other, for this was a courting pair performing their wedding dance. They ran through the swathes of primroses, violets and other early woodland flowers before assailing a large beech tree and bounding off through the canopy until lost to view.

The red squirrel was not the only rusty-coloured animal to pass in front of my eyes, for no woodland is without its resident red fox. Our most adaptable native mammal, the fox occurs in every imaginable habitat; from the open moors where the red grouse live amongst the heather, to the inner city streets where it ignores the passing pedestrians with an aloofness unique to its character. The foxes that often trotted daintily past the woodpeckers were very different from the scruffy, rope-tailed and mangy individuals that many city dwellers encounter. They were crisp and pristine in appearance, like the woodpeckers they lived alongside, and they had full brushes that swept the ground behind them like feather dusters. While they posed no risk to woodpeckers nesting in the trees, they would certainly willingly take any individuals unfortunate to land on the ground, either foraging adults or youngsters on their maiden flights.

The great spotted woodpeckers in County Wicklow have spread from the British population 140 kilometres across the Irish Sea, and it is interesting that several of the woodpeckers' avian neighbours here in Ireland may also have originated from the British countryside.

The common buzzard, widespread across Ireland in times long past but latterly confined to Rathlin Island, off the County Antrim coast, almost certainly due to the uncontrolled use of poison on farmland, has now increased nationally and is breeding in almost every county. The Wicklow population, one of the first to establish itself outside Northern Ireland, was derived from birds that wandered here from Wales. This is hardly surprising, as on a clear day they would have been able to see the Irish coastline as they soared over the mountains of Snowdonia. Although the pioneer buzzards were initially far slower than the woodpeckers to colonize, they are now a familiar sight across the country and can even be seen soaring regularly over Dublin City. A pair of buzzards bred in the same woodland as the woodpeckers, although I never located their nest, mainly because they are late breeders and I was no longer regularly visiting the woodland by the time they were feeding their young. Their mewing cries as they circled in the blue skies over the woodpeckers' nest formed a daily soundtrack and were a welcome indication of the ability of birds to colonize new territory when suitable conditions arise. Although a top predator, they pose no risk whatsoever to the nesting woodpeckers. As our largest native bird of prey, they have neither the agility nor the speed to capture a woodpecker bounding rapidly through the woodland canopies.

The Avonmore River flowing through the heart of the woodland was home to another Welsh colonist, and a most unusual one at that, the goosander. This is a member of the duck family with which most people in Ireland are completely unfamiliar. They are present in such small numbers that the distribution maps in many bird books show them as being absent from Ireland. The total Irish population is probably less than fifty pairs, the majority of which are found in County Wicklow on the Avonmore River and its tributaries. Streamlined like a submarine, they swim low to the water, the males' black and white plumage blending perfectly with the dappled foam flecked riffles as the river cuts its course through the trees. Their dark bottle-green heads sport a short shaggy crest while a long, thin, blood red bill pierces the water as it torpedoes through in search of fish.

Goosanders share a most unusual trait with woodpeckers, although they bear no relation to them. Confined primarily to

Wicklow's glaciated lakes and fast-flowing mountain rivers, they nest in holes in trees along the banks in the surrounding woodland. Unlike the woodpeckers, which excavate their own nesting chambers, the furtive goosander uses natural holes and cavities in the trunks of old trees. The scarcity of such natural nest sites is the most likely reason for the continuing restricted population, which shows little sign of any increase in numbers. It is hard to imagine two more different birds than these sharing the same woodland nesting habits.

The great spotted woodpecker is only one of a diverse range of species inhabiting the same woodland, all of which have adapted to the harsh conditions that the Wicklow Mountains enforce on their lifestyles. Rivers rise, fall, and even freeze, trees are uprooted and moorland lies blanketed in snow...

Yet, the enigmatic species of the Wicklow Mountains endure.

7.
SHORTENING DAYS

IT WAS LATE NOVEMBER when at last I returned to the woods where the woodpeckers had raised and cared for their family, that is until Red and Black had tragically met their demise. Winter is the most difficult time of year in which to watch woodpeckers in their natural habitat. There is usually no drumming to be heard, and calls are limited to the odd sporadic *Kik* whenever a foraging bird becomes aware of a potential predator. It is possible to walk for several hours through cold and bare winter woodland without encountering a single woodpecker, whereas just a few months previously the same area would have provided several sightings within an hour, and more if a nest happened to be nearby. Fleeting and frustrating glimpses become the norm, with a bird suddenly calling and bounding further away into the depths of the wood before binoculars can even be raised to allow identification of its age or sex.

On my November walk, frustration grew as my body temperature fell; if the purpose of my excursion had been actually to observe woodpeckers, then it began to feel more and more pointless a venture with every extra step I took. Fortunately, there were many other birds in the woods to enjoy while I sought my quarry; roving flocks of blue and great tits flitted amongst the leaf litter, while accompanying goldcrests and coal tits gave their high-pitched calls as they foraged in the bare branches above. Looking upwards at these restless feathered sprites, I saw the canopy of russet autumn was now replaced with an intricate, fine, black web of interlocking branches against a blue sky.

Despite the tireless searching, even achieving a fleeting glimpse of a woodpecker amongst the trees at this time of year is a challenge. Often, a bird would call from a hundred or so metres away in the depths of the wood. However, by the time I could cut off from the track and weave my way through the russet layers of bracken and the decaying, tangled summer growth of bramble, bilberry and horsetail, I would encounter nothing but the deepening silence of winter.

Part of the reason for the woodpeckers' elusiveness during winter is that they often range over a larger area than merely their established breeding territory. The young birds have also dispersed by this stage, although having now moulted their crimson crowns they have become virtually indistinguishable from the adults. However, young woodpeckers entering their first winter often retain a paler shade of scarlet on the undertail, more like a pinkish wash than the vibrant scarlet shown by the adult birds. This feature is retained until the following feather moult, often enabling some individuals at nest holes to be aged, albeit tentatively.

A particular feature of woodpecker behaviour, which seems predominantly confined to the winter months is what I refer to as 'pinnacle calling'. A bird will suddenly appear on the extreme top of a bare tree, on the highest and usually thinnest branch; indeed, its chosen perch is often not even worthy of being called a branch, but more correctly a twig. It then perches precariously, its weight causing the twig to bend and swing like a swaying cobra, all the while calling loudly and continuously, often for several minutes. Then the bird will take off, but instead of flying back down into the canopy it will tower up in the sky, bounding across open countryside until lost to view. On one occasion, using a map afterwards, I measured the distance I had followed a woodpecker while in flight: it was over 500 metres and still I didn't see it land. This behaviour can be encountered anywhere; in woods, villages and even gardens. For a generally secretive and seemingly elusive bird it seems quite out of character for it to perch so obviously and in such an exposed position for such lengthy periods of time and deliberately drawing attention to itself through its incessant calling; doubtless a hungry sparrowhawk would quickly avail of such an opportunity if it happened to be nearby.

In some ways this behaviour is reminiscent of that of a completely different and highly specialised species of bird, namely the bearded reedling. This extremely scarce species, which is the sole European representative of a family which mainly occurs in the grasslands of Central and Eastern Asia, only began breeding in Ireland in 2010 after an absence of more than a quarter of a century. It is roughly the size of a pied wagtail and lives in large extensive reed beds along the east and southeast coast of Ireland. Only about thirty or forty pairs are estimated to breed in Ireland. The male is a vibrantly-coloured bird with a small, neat, bright yellow bill and a blue-grey head, sporting a pristine and distinguished gringo-style black moustache. His tawny-orange body contrasts with irregular meandering black stripes on his wings. Like wagtails, his tail is as long as his body, and it is also the same tawny-orange colour hue. Bearded reedlings are usually hard to see amongst the swaying reeds to which they are more or less restricted, and their loud metallic *Ping* calls are often all that betrays their presence.

Sometimes groups of bearded reedlings will cling to the wispy feathered plumes of the tallest reeds, calling *Ping... Ping* loudly before launching themselves high into the clear sky and gradually disappearing from view, merging with other faint dots on the horizon.

It is believed that this is how they expand their range and colonise new areas, flying high in order to see what lies far ahead. I could not help wondering whether similar behaviour is what enabled the great spotted woodpeckers in Wales to fly across the Irish Sea with the certainty of finding land and not just endless ocean and probable death. Yet the great spotted woodpeckers that I have observed behaving in this manner did not seem to me to have been trying to expand their range. Possibly, they were exploring new parts of their territory in advance of the coming breeding season, or perhaps they were young birds searching out new territories.

The male great spotted woodpecker usually maintains a presence, albeit minimal, in his breeding territory throughout the winter. Sometimes this is limited to just appearing at the nest hole before going to roost at dusk, often as the planet Venus appears shining in the darkening sky. Sometimes either member of the pair may pass through the territory during the day, travelling in search of richer food sources. With the arrival of winter, a new food source, in the form of garden bird feeders, now tempts many of the woodpeckers away from their normal habitat during the harshest months of the year.

Ireland is a nation of bird-lovers and the volume of bird food sold nationwide each winter is staggering. Hundreds of tonnes of peanuts and seed are imported annually and used to feed our garden birds. While some woodpeckers are fortunate to have access to peanut feeders all year round, other birds are not so fortunate and many gardens feeders are only made available during the winter months. At this time of year, because birds are no longer territorial, they will fly considerable distances to visit peanut feeders and as a result I often encountered woodpeckers in areas well outside their normal habitat, such as alongside roads or in housing estates. In many cases these 'out of character' sightings can be linked to a nearby peanut feeder.

The gradually increasing population of woodpeckers in Ireland has been slow to avail of peanut feeders being present in many gardens. Just over the water, however, they are common visitors to bird feeders, as indeed they are across much of northern Europe. In many cases the

Irish woodpeckers visit feeders more during the breeding season when they have hungry families to feed. Possibly the density of woodpeckers in County Wicklow, until recently, was sufficiently low that there was no competition for food and therefore no need to visit feeders, since their large territories more than adequately met their needs. With numbers now increasing, however, they are becoming more regular a sight alongside the familiar blue tits and robins, which also avail of our kindness.

It is tempting to think that watching woodpeckers on peanut feeders is an easy task, not to mention far more civilized than spending hours in midge-infested woods with cramping joints or frozen fingers to contend with. The excellent photographs often shared over the internet showing arched woodpeckers suspended like bananas under peanut feeders add weight to this attractive image. Sadly, more often than not, this is an aspiring dream and is a far cry from reality. Watching the multitude of tits, sparrows and finches crowding my bird feeders during the early winter mornings, from the warmth of my kitchen window with my steaming mug of coffee in hand, is a morning ritual in which I revel. My feeders are only about ten metres away, and I don't need binoculars to enjoy the frantic spectacle. Robins, blackbirds, dunnocks, house sparrows, chaffinches and blue tits all jostle and fight for space like city commuters on an escalator in a train station... but not the woodpecker, no not him.

He will sometimes visit early in the morning, before the low winter sun has even crossed the horizon and the garden is still bathed in the predawn glow of a winter's full moon. The house sparrows, all clustered on the feeder, scatter in every direction as, silently, he swoops in and lands. Hanging upside down from the bottom of the feeder, like a black and white banana, his tail pointed up at the sky on one side and his bill on the other, he casts a wary eye about his surroundings. One careless movement from myself in the darkness of the unlit kitchen, or indeed a sudden bark from my dog, and he will be gone. Due to the woodpecker's larger size, other birds do not approach the feeder while he feeds, stabbing at the peanuts through the wire mesh. Usually, even if undisturbed, after only a few brief moments he will bound back into the treetops and slip away. Great spotted woodpeckers do not seem to rely on garden feeders during the winter months, and certainly not in the manner that some pairs appear to depend on them during the breeding season. Following the dispersal of the youngsters in early autumn, the population of woodpeckers in Wicklow probably still remains so low that competition for food is not an issue. This does not seem to be the case in Great Britain, where the woodpecker population density is far higher and woodpeckers are more frequent visitors to garden bird feeders.

Although most winter encounters with woodpeckers are unexpected and usually brief, they provide some memorable sightings. One bitterly cold December morning, I was walking along the edge of a wood when a familiar sounding *Kik* reached my ears. The temperature the previous night had dropped to minus five, and the early morning air had that stinging clarity that made my earlobes ache, making that woodpecker's call sound all the more crisp. The sun, still lurking below the horizon, had reached out its first rays to touch the topmost branches of a row of ash trees, bathing them with a soft golden wash. There amongst them sat a female great spotted woodpecker, her back towards me as she pecked intently on the green lichens covering the branches. When she turned around, all of her white underparts were suffused with gold and glowed as the rising sun reflected off her body. She paused momentarily in her endeavours, squinting as the disc of the sun finally emerged and flowed across the winter landscape, causing tendrils of mist to rise from the frozen grass.

When great spotted woodpeckers first began to colonize Ireland, several years before breeding was proven, some freshly-excavated holes were discovered during the winter months. When woodpeckers arrive in a habitat previously uninhabited by other woodpeckers they often excavate 'bolt holes' in which to roost. Unlike the fully excavated nesting chamber, these holes do not extend as far down into the tree but rather stop after several centimetres. The woodpecker can roost relatively safely inside these, although a predator could probably still reach in and catch one if it was determined enough. Once breeding had occurred, and when fully-excavated nest holes were scattered about the woods, the woodpeckers opted to roost in these, the greater depth offering more security. As a result, bolt-holes became much scarcer, as the need for them had lessened.

The male of an established pair often chooses to roost alone in the previous season's nest hole during the winter months. Whether his mate roosts in a different nest hole nearby or simply roosts while clinging to the bark of a tree I was unable to determine. Watching woodpeckers going to roost is a challenge, and often a fruitless one. Because they roam around a larger area during the winter months, they can often still be foraging up to a kilometre away when the sun slides down behind the darkening mountaintops and dusk starts to creep in. Sitting motionless in the woods, at this hour, during the darkest month, the winter chill enters one's bones surprisingly quickly, no matter how well prepared one may be.

As dusk encroaches, blackbirds can be heard calling *Chink... Chink* for quite some time before, finally, they settle down to roost. The first woodcock of the evening can occasionally be glimpsed flying out from the depths of the leaf-littered undergrowth to feed in surrounding fields and in the margins of the woods. Unlike their roding display flights during the early summer, when their curious *qu-zik* call carries through the air, these winter flightings[12] to nearby feeding grounds are usually conducted silently, except for the whispering of their wings.

It is usually at this stage in the closing of the evening that it begins to feel as though the journey has possibly been pointless. The black circle of the nesting hole is now almost impossible to discern against the darkening silhouette of the nesting tree, and the growing light of the Poacher's Lantern[13] above the horizon shows that dusk is ending and darkness is commencing... and then movement. The male great spotted woodpecker flies completely silently, seemingly out of

---

[12] Flightings: Wildfowlers term for the flight line a game species makes between its roosting site and feeding location.
[13] Poacher's Lantern: The Full Moon.

nowhere, to land directly at the entrance hole. He pauses momentarily, tilting his head sideways, before quickly shuffling through the aperture and becoming lost to view. Occasionally, if fortune permits, a glimpse of red on the back of the head can be seen as he squeezes into the hole, showing that it is indeed the male. I find it interesting that the woodpecker waits until so late in the evening before he goes to roost, since so many familiar birds, such as starlings, blackbirds and jackdaws, can be seen doing so over an hour before the woodpecker makes his last-minute flight.

Many years ago, I saw a great tit regularly go to roost in a hollow metal pipe, and it was always almost dark before he would squeeze his way inside so that he was merely a silhouette, with no indication of plumage or markings visible. Like the woodpecker, the great tit is a hole-nesting species, and although I have seen them nesting in old woodpecker nest holes, I have yet to see any roost in one.

The winter months can be a challenging time for the great spotted woodpecker, but nothing lasts for ever...

And, as the sun starts to increase in its elevation, spring returns.

8.
RETURN TO THE WOODS

FEBRUARY 2016 ONCE again found me deep in the woods, surveying the territory of the spanish chestnut woodpeckers, after an absence of over six months. The weather during the previous winter had been contrastingly different from that of the year before. Storm after storm had raged across the country, bringing trees down and causing rivers to flood, and turning what was usually deciduous woodland into scenes reminiscent of Arkansas and its flooded forests; the last known home of the now extinct ivory-billed woodpecker.

With the arrival of February, the storms had abated, allowing a window in which to assess how the birds had fared during the winter. I was relieved to see that the nesting tree, the spanish chestnut, was still standing, despite the fact that two nearby beeches had succumbed to the storms and were now lying broken, only metres away from it. The whole woodland was littered with casualties from the battling wind.

Broken boughs and branches told of a challenging winter and made me wonder whether my birds had survived.

Although winter keeps its harsh grip on the Wicklow uplands far later than it can in the lowlands, spring was already underway in many parts of the country. Birds such as blackbirds and robins were already incubating eggs, but here at these higher elevations it would be several more weeks before any true indication of spring would be evident.

Although the storms had now abated, the weather was still dull, overcast and cold. My first two visits failed to produce any sign of the woodpeckers. Great spotted woodpeckers do not like adverse weather conditions and generally sit tight, doing very little other than feeding until the weather changes.

However, even in such inclement conditions, other birds still carry on foraging. Redwings flew over the treetops like swarms of arrowheads, their high pitched *tseeee-p* calls sounding like the wind through feathered fletchings[14], before being truncated as though hitting the trees. Sometimes fieldfares joined them, uttering harsh nasal *chack-chack* calls, often interspersed with other random high-pitched whistles and squeaks. Both these species of thrush are winter visitors to Ireland from colder climes, to which they return as the sun climbs ever higher in the late spring skies.

I sometimes stayed in the woods until dusk at that time of year, hoping to catch a glimpse of the male woodpecker going to roost. Though the woodland may have been bereft of sightings throughout the day, the male could simply fly in as the light was fading. It was a pleasure to be there alone in the fading light watching the circadian rhythms of the woodland inhabitants guiding their behaviour, like a theatrical performance unfolding.

Woodpigeons, fat from gorging on ivy berries, flew into the tallest beech trees, crashing into the canopy like an avalanche of stones. They flapped around noisily before settling down to roost, their bills

---

[14] Fletchings: The vanes on an arrow shaft which keep the flight true.

drooping onto their dusky pink breasts. Safe from terrestrial predators, they slept easily in their lofty towers.

Woodcock, those cryptic denizens of the woodlands, dashed silently overhead as I watched them 'flighting' from their daytime roosts amongst the decaying leaf litter that covered the woodland floor. These snipe-like birds, rarely seen by the casual observer, were heading to the nearby rides and fields to spend the night probing in the ground with their long, sensitive bills in search of earthworms. Their rounded wings, hunched shoulders and lumbering flight created a spectral sight against the darkening blue of the nautical twilight[15]. In a few weeks' time these Woodcock would begin their nightly roding, where they fly above the canopy while uttering a strange, high-pitched *quisip* call, interspersed with low, deep, guttural *gurk-gurk-gurk* sounds. Nature has so much to offer, far more than any man-made amusements. It often frequently infuriates me when I realise how little time we are granted to explore it: work and sleep occupy so much of our lives that life's truly important moments are often lost without us even knowing.

Finally, in late February, there was a break from the low pressure weather systems that had been affecting the country for weeks. A high pressure system centred over Ireland, wind ceased, the sun came out and the temperature plummeted. Night temperatures fell to −4°c, and daytime figures struggled to rise above 5 or 6°c. At the first opportunity, I headed to the woods. It was a pleasure to be there, woodpeckers or not. Being so early in the year, I was unable to drive along the woodland tracks to the nest site due to flooding, so I parked some distance away and walked. It was shortly after sunrise and the sun was just barely over the surrounding hills. Winter woodland early on a frosty morning is magical, taking you into a world where you almost feel like an intruder in an environment that is to the woodpecker what the world of steel and concrete is to us humans.

---

[15] Nautical twilight: This is the second of the three phases of twilight, preceded by civil twilight and followed by astronomical twilight. It occurs when the geometric centre of the sun is between six and twelve degrees below the horizon.

As I walked along, lost in the crunching of my footsteps in the ice-covered tracks, I watched my breath steaming in front of me and wondered if this was another futile search. Although long-lived, up to eight or nine years, woodpeckers are still mortal (as I knew all too well), and either of the previous year's pair could have succumbed to weather, predators or just simply old age. Was it a vain hope that the territory would be occupied by another pair?

The thought had barely crossed my mind when the crystal stillness of the frosty air was shattered by a burst of drumming; a woodpecker proclaiming to all challengers that this territory was indeed occupied.

I stopped with a relieved smile on my face. Had I been accompanied by anyone, I probably would have 'high-fived' them with gusto, no doubt to their astonishment. Why was I so relieved? Knowing that a new season lay ahead of me in which I would share the intimacies of one of nature's most specialised birds and that some of the remaining questions I had might be answered, I would once more enjoy spending time alone in the woods with nothing but nature to keep me company. These thoughts put a smile on my face that no amount of the stress and uncertainty that comes with daily life could remove.

Following the sound of the drumming, I soon located a bird high in the bare trees; a quick glimpse of red on its nape and I knew it was a male. He seemed oblivious to my presence, completely focused on listening for any reply that might indicate a rival. After each burst of drumming, he paused and turned his head to one side, seemingly to listen for a reply and accurately pinpoint its direction and source. Today, at least, the woods stayed silent in response to his proclamation.

I arrived one morning early in March to find the woodland in a state of chaos – at least it was chaos from a woodpecker's point of view. There were birds calling agitatedly *KI... KIK... KIK* from several parts of the wood, and other rattling and churring calls were coming sporadically from the treetops. I quietly sat down against a tree and watched the bare branches, silhouetted against the blue sky. It took me a while to figure out how many birds were actually present, as I noted in my diary at the time:

'... *09.20 – Just arrived, birds flying everywhere –*
certainly three – more likely four, possibly five...'

The chaos was testosterone-driven and the dispute was over real
estate. This small patch of woodland was, to my eyes, scarcely any
different from all the other surrounding woods, yet apparently it
was prime territory and had caught the beady eyes of other roving
woodpeckers. And it wasn't just the woodland that was the target;
the invading forces seemed to be focusing very much on the spanish
chestnut tree itself.

The established pair was very proactive in its defence against
an intruding male, who seemed to be focused on trying to land on
the tree itself, as though this would give him a certain claim, in the
same manner as a mountaineer struggles towards an unconquered
peak to plant his flag on the summit. His mere presence in their
territory was cause enough for alarm, but his action of trying to
land on the tree was driving the established pair into a frenzy
almost beyond control.

As the intruder flew through the leafless canopy, the resident
male was hot on his tail, screaming frantically *keeeeek... keeeeek...
keeeeek*. The desperate urgency and shrillness of his cries ripped
through this quiet glade like a screaming klaxon on a diving
submarine. 'Intruder Alert... Intruder Alert' was being broadcast
throughout the woodland for anyone with understanding. As the two
males approached the spanish chestnut tree, the female flew in from
the opposite direction in a panicked attempt to head the intruder
off. She blocked his flight and landed, whereupon she immediately
started drumming with an intensity that was only matched by the
frantic look in her eyes. The two males shot past like piebald bullets,
their high-pitched screams trailing after them. Glancing over her
shoulder, the female took off and flew after them, uttering her loud
trilling call. A few minutes later the whole procedure was repeated,
as the invading male desperately tried to reach the nest tree, all the
time with the resident male screaming indignantly behind him. The

female was trying to keep pace, while stopping to land on every tree she could to hammer out a warning burst before frantically flying on after the distantly disappearing males.

At one stage while I was watching these three birds, a fourth suddenly called to my left. I never managed to see this bird, which makes its appearance on the scene all the more intriguing. Was it a third male perhaps, or was it the mate of the intruding male? This latter prospect is especially interesting, as it would suggest that a bonded pair had formed without establishing a territory and was roaming the area in search of one.

It was all becoming frustratingly confusing, and this wasn't set to change. A few moments later, a bird was heard drumming even further back in the woods. I suspected that what might be happening was that there were two pairs plus a single unattached male moving across the territories and trying either to stake a claim or to take one of the females as his mate.

Interestingly, swallows show a somewhat similar behaviour. An unpaired male, known as a 'rogue male', will fly up to a nest with chicks in it and kill the young by throwing them out of the nest onto the ground below. He then mates with the female, unbeknownst to the resident male, before moving on, leaving the paired male to rear the offspring of the rogue when they hatch. I couldn't help wondering whether male woodpeckers use a similar strategy.

Watching woodpeckers early in the year, during courtship, is much easier, if somewhat less rewarding, than watching birds at the nest. In general, the birds are higher in the canopy and are not disturbed by an observer's presence, meaning one can sit completely out in the open. This enables you to follow birds around the territory with ease. However, as I had discovered during the previous season, a hide situated near the nest allows excellent opportunities for more detailed study at a time when the birds are easily alarmed and will not tolerate an observer's presence.

Although last year's hide was a great success, I knew that this season I would want to build it even closer to the nest and also in such a manner that would enable me to look out in all directions, including overhead. I had felt frustrated on many occasions during the previous year, as the birds frequently chose to feed in a blind spot, something which I really wanted to avoid this year. Although I hadn't actually seen any nest hole excavation or inspection of previous nest holes, I was pretty confident that my pair's robust defence of the tree against intruders was a strong indication that they would nest here again.

With my decision made, I was keen to get started as soon as possible, rather than miss any nest-building behaviour. With the weather having now improved to the point where I could drive on the woodland tracks, I headed off along the Avonmore River with a forest of timber protruding from the boot of the car. I arrived late in the afternoon during the first week of March, my car laden with the most varied mix of equipment I had ever subjected it to. Fourteen large two metre-length planks with the bark still on the outside, three posts, eight large bathroom towels, ten metres of black silage wrap, numerous assorted small pieces of timber, a large coil of rope, bamboo canes, spades, a pickaxe, hammers, saws, drills, nails and most importantly of all… my trusty Swiss Army knife.

Not just any Swiss Army knife, either. The *Swisschamp* is one of the latest models derived from the original Swiss Army knife, which was designed over one hundred years ago, and boasting nineteen tools providing thirty-three functions. Numerous occasions had arisen in the course of the previous year, both during construction and in the daily use of the hide, which required its use, and several observations of woodpecker behaviour in Ireland would probably have gone unrecorded save for this essential item!

All through the winter, I had mused over the construction of my hide and the observations that it would hopefully reveal. I was really looking forward to the prospect of a whole season of nest study and I wanted this hide to be faultless.

I had reached the end of the track and parked the car when the realisation hit home: the nest site was about one hundred metres from the car and up a steep sloping track, and I was transporting the gear by myself. Carrying hammers and small lengths of timber presents little challenge; however, the roughhewn timber was a different story. Each plank was an ungainly 2m in length, about 10cm wide and weighed about 20kg, and there were fourteen of them – 280kg of timber to be carried uphill.

Why was I using this timber? Simply because I had got it for free from a local sawmill. The planks were the 'trimmings' taken from the complete trunks to make them square for thinner and more precise plank milling. As a result, they varied in thickness from 3cm to 6cm, as they followed the curve of the tree. As well as being free, to my mind they also looked more natural than planed wood and would hopefully blend better into the woodland.

I carried the planks up one at a time. By number ten, my enthusiasm was waning, to say the least. My shoulder was rubbed raw from their weight and my foot was throbbing where I had fallen and dropped a plank square on my toes – the shout I let out probably sent every fox, deer and woodpecker in the area running for cover. I conveniently decided at this point that maybe I didn't need every plank to be brought up straight away. After all, what if I needed to move the hide? Or suppose I had too many planks? It would be pointless to lug them all up if I had to carry them back down.

Despite all my musings over the hide construction, during the darkest months of the year, I now realised I didn't have a blueprint for this hide – I was building by the seat of my pants. Out of breath and with a red face dripping with sweat, I offloaded the last planks and stacked them neatly beside the track. I then rolled the towels and small tools in the silage wrap, tied a rope around them and the other end around my waist, grabbed the posts and bamboo canes and set off up through the woods like an explorer across the Antarctic, dragging my sleigh behind me. It might only have been an oakwood in County Wicklow, but watching these woodpeckers was beginning to seem like the transantarctic expedition during the 1950s.[16]

---

[16] Commonwealth Trans-Antarctic Expedition 1955–58.

Two hours after I had parked the car, I finally arrived at the nest site with the final load. In all this time I hadn't seen or heard a woodpecker, but this didn't surprise or concern me. When it comes to nest-related activities, Woodpeckers are most active in the morning, and the territory was large so they could happily have been feeding undisturbed in a different part of the wood. It was very early in their breeding season and my activities posed no threat of disturbance to them.

It was now time for my second challenge of the day. I didn't know exactly where I was going to build the hide, mainly because I didn't know which side of the tree they were planning to nest on, but also because it is only when the materials are laid out can you see how they might fit into the lie of the land. One thing that I did know was that I wanted to be closer to the tree than I had been during the previous season. I also wanted the hide to be bigger.

Last year's hide had been located to the north-east of the nest tree, and I had used an oak as a solid corner post onto which I attached the timber-framed hide. Another large oak tree stood about 10m east of the nest tree. Standing alongside it, I found I could see three nest holes: that from the previous season, which had also been used in 2013, the 2014 nest hole and the most recently excavated, and the as-yet unused, nest hole from the previous year. This nest hole was directly facing me while the others were on a side profile. If the pair used this nest hole, I was in for an exciting 'in your face' season of activity. My only concern was that a nearby earthen bank ran alongside the northern face of the tree. If I constructed a hide here, I would struggle to observe anything on that side; I hoped that it wouldn't completely hinder me, but only time would tell. Although it was still too early to confirm which nest hole the woodpeckers would use, I decided the light was good from this angle, the panorama of the surrounding woodland was excellent and there would be plenty of activity on all sides of the tree. Anyway, I could always build another hide on the other side if they settled on that aspect of the tree – it would just mean another 280kg of wood to be dragged uphill!

I decided to only construct the bare skeleton of the hide at this stage, since I expected to be carrying out my observations in the general area for at least another couple of weeks, rather than just in this specific glade. I drove a couple of posts into the earthen bank and attached several planks to the tree, temporarily fixing them to the post at the other end. I now knew from the previous year how important it was during the building of the hide to ensure that the viewing areas are in the most advantageous locations, so the next thing I did was to make a seat. Having spent most of the previous season cramped on a wet piece of bark, I wanted more comfort this time round.

As soon as I had my seat fixed up and foot-well excavated, I was able to see where the various planks would go, simply by looking around and visualizing where the birds would be feeding, flying and most importantly, where they would be visible on the nesting tree. Once the framework and the front of the hide had been erected, I decided to leave the rest of the construction, roof and walls until a later date, when the birds had given an indication of which nest hole they intended using.

As I was packing away all the tools and remaining kit into the silage wrap and securing it with rope, I heard a loud *KIK* from nearby, and I looked up just in time to see a woodpecker flying into a nearby tree. I hoped he liked what he saw and wasn't looking for planning permission. The sun was now setting, so I left the area quite promptly, as in all likelihood the bird that I saw may have been preparing to roost in one of the nest holes and I didn't want to disturb his routine. Satisfied that progress was being made, I decided to call it a day and headed back home along the river. As dusk drew in, a number of sika deer came to graze in the birch scrub beside the car, and I heard the welcome melody of a song thrush fluting in the trees overhead, alongside a blackbird. Spring was slowly creeping towards the Wicklow Mountains at long last.

By this stage, much of the territorial displaying had finished and woodpecker sightings were starting to become more focused in and around the nesting tree. It was now time to finish the hide and take up a more permanent watch.

Even the most enthusiastic observer will succumb to cramps, midges and stiffness, so comfort is paramount during long observations. I knew from the previous season that I had missed several interesting moments because I had to move awkwardly or simply was unable to see due to being in such a cramped position.

At this point the hide looked quite bizarre, with the framework erected using the large planks and a few cross planks for the roof. As I needed several large openings, I had fitted the planks on the front and side in such a manner that every alternate row was missing, giving the effect of a zebra-crossing. I now nailed the towels on the inside of the walls, effectively lining the inside of the hide. Using my Swiss Army knife, while sitting on the stool in the hide, I now simply cut a small slit in the towels at any point I felt I might need to look out, then I fitted a safety pin to close it.

The day I had chosen to carry out these finishing touches was incredibly windy; not that this was unusual in the Wicklow Mountains, but it made the remaining task a bit more challenging. I laid out the silage wrap and doubled it over to form a large heavy sheet which would act as a roof. Doing this on my own in a strong wind was incredibly frustrating, but trying to nail it to one side of the tree and stretch it tightly across the hide to the other side nearly thwarted me completely. I was in the middle of trying to stop the wind from tearing the plastic off (whereupon it would no doubt end up tangled in the barbed wire around the distant fields – sadly, a ubiquitous sight of the Irish countryside) when a loud *KIK... KIK... KIK* alerted me – I had visitors and the place was in a state!

I quickly weighed the plastic down with rocks as a temporary measure and then dived inside out of sight. I opened one of the safety pin latches and sat looking out across the silent glade. Within seconds, the male woodpecker landed on a short spur just 5m from where I sat and started drumming – the noise at this range was incredible. I had often believed I was close when watching them earlier in the year, but now I realised how far removed I had really been. It wasn't just the actual noise; I could *feel* the sound and the way it reverberated down the tree, into the soil and out across the woodland.

The sun was shining on the spur where he perched and I could see every detail of his plumage, right down to his zebra-striped tail. He was completely relaxed and sat contentedly after a few bursts of drumming, his eyes half-closed in the sunshine as he contemplated his woodland realm. After several minutes, he suddenly sat up alert, looked around, called twice and flew high up into the canopy. Another *KIK* sounded from the topmost bough of the spanish chestnut – there was the female, having arrived unnoticed. She called again and from deep within the wood the male answered distantly. She took off and disappeared into the trees – they were gone.

I sat there motionless; I had been totally absorbed in the event. I had spent the previous season watching the same tree from a hide further back, so the experience wasn't completely new, but moving that extra few metres had brought me into a whole new world. I didn't need binoculars or telescopes anymore. Instead of merely watching the woodpeckers, as I had done in the previous season, I now felt I was living with them and, more importantly, my presence did not seem to be affecting their behaviour in any way that I could see.

This brief encounter, lasting less than a minute, raised a whole series of questions, any of which could keep an ornithologist occupied for years. In decades gone by, early naturalists used hides as a means to watch wildlife in the understanding that the birds wouldn't know the observer was there and hence would behave naturally. Some naturalists used to recommend being accompanied by a friend to a hide, since it was assumed birds couldn't count and if they saw a person walking away from the hide they wouldn't realise that a second person had remained behind and therefore would not modify their behaviour. However, on this occasion, the male woodpecker had seen me before I had even been aware of his presence. He had called to alert me to his arrival and had presumably watched me then move into the hide, yet as soon as I was inside he stopped calling and approached to within metres of where he had last seen me.

This event made me wonder, and not for the first time, about the problem of trying to figure out how much awareness a brain smaller than a walnut is actually capable of processing. Is it just a case of 'out of sight, out of mind' and that the bird simply lives in the present, with no thought for past or future? Do any behavioural traits that suggest otherwise constitute anything more than that unquantifiable catch-all referred to as 'instinct'?

I returned to my work with renewed vigour, and in a short space of time had the plastic sheet fixed into place with batons to form a waterproof roof. Unfortunately, I had constructed the hide on a slope, so had to excavate a considerable hole into the bank while inside to ensure there was sufficient room to use a tripod for my telescope, as well as to ensure that I had sufficient space quickly to manoeuvre from side to side, depending on the activity of the birds at the time. A final few bits of timber were fitted as rough basic shelves and I was done. While hardly worthy of the phrase 'home from home', I expected to spend a considerable amount of time here in the coming months, especially once the young had hatched, but all that was in the future – my immediate goal was to watch woodpecker pre-incubation behaviour, an aspect of their life cycle I had barely covered during my previous years' observations.

Satisfied with my progress, several journeys were made back to the car to return the tools and unused materials – thankfully it was all downhill this time. Once again, darkness was approaching as I headed off along the winding tree-lined track beside the river. A new chapter was beginning – I was looking forward to the next day.

The end of March also brought an end to the settled period of weather, as Storm 'Jake' roared across the country and left a trail of destruction in its wake. Yet more trees came down in the woodpeckers' territory, and the sun disappeared behind dark cumulus clouds for days on end. Many birds dislike weather such as this, but seemingly none more so than woodpeckers. During this time the activities of the birds around the nest site were quite diminished and erratic. Often it was only occasional calls that gave away their presence.

Unlike many other birds, woodpeckers rarely feel solid ground beneath their feet, given that much of their time is spent on the side of a tree. During weather as stormy as we had been experiencing, this must be quite difficult for them. A woodpecker's bill is a precision instrument, and trying to wield it whilst being buffeted by storm force wind must be a big challenge.

It is often said during experiments that negative results are as important as positive; however, there is negative and there is pointless! Despite my enthusiasm and determination, the torrential rain that followed for several days rendered any effort at tracking woodpeckers futile. The river burst its banks again, and once more the woods succumbed to an inundation of water. Many of the local early-nesting birds along the river, such as the dipper, must find the fluctuating water levels a hindrance to their breeding. It makes food sources inaccessible at a crucial time of year.

The weather in early April carried on as March had finished – cold, blustery and generally quite wet. Most days spent in the hide were dull and overcast. This is often a quiet month for noting sightings in the woodpecker diary, which contrasts with that of other resident birds, many of which have by then reached peak breeding activity. March is the peak month for defending territories, for drumming and for watching territorial disputes and nuptial flights. By contrast, April seems to be a month of waiting: waiting for egg-laying and incubation. It is followed by the busiest month of all – May, and chick-rearing. But during early and mid-April, most sightings are simply of birds feeding quietly in the trees. I had hoped that this year would be the one in which they might excavate a new nest hole, conveniently in front of me, but as yet there seemed to be no indications of any such activity.

By the middle of April I still didn't know where they intended to nest, or even if they would be using an established nest hole or excavating a new one. Because of this, I divided my time between watching the spanish chestnut tree and walking around the woods looking at other trees for any signs of fresh excavations. Both of the woodpeckers seemed very intolerant of disturbance in their territory at this stage and became very vocal if disturbed. As I watched from the cover of the holly bush, where I often sat before nesting commenced, I always knew when other people were passing through the woods, because the woodpeckers would become very agitated, calling loudly and flying from tree to tree. Despite being April, the trees were still quite bare, for the oak is usually the last of our native trees to begin unfurling its leaves and a full leaf canopy in these woodlands does not usually occur until the end of May. However, when the woodland was undisturbed, hours often passed with very little indication that the birds were even present...

> *April 6 (08.55–11.30)*
> *Very cold and blustery morning, recent rain now cleared. Trees creaking loudly in wind making it hard to listen for birds. Bird called at 10:10 distantly from south of tree.*

Two days later, things hadn't improved much...

> *April 8 (09.30–12.30)*
> *Dull, overcast and cold but little or no wind.*
> *Watched upper part of glade from under cypress tree.*
> *09.56: Bird called twice from 100m due east.*
> *10.40: Single burst of drumming, very close. Didn't see bird.*
> *11.03: 'Rattling' calls heard several times, 50m due south.*

Given the scarcity of sightings during this period and the continuing uncomfortable weather, it was often tempting to 'jump ship' and just wait until the birds were feeding young and then recommence my watching. However, the woodland wasn't completely devoid of activity at this time of year and there was always something to enjoy. One surprising neighbour of the woodpeckers was a pair of mistle thrushes.

The mistle thrush is the largest of our native thrushes, with a proud upright stance and boldly spotted underparts. Usually it prefers open parks and fields, where it can be seen hopping across the short grass in a manner that reminded me of sika deer as they bounce away on their stiff pogostick-like legs when disturbed. Here in the Wicklow Mountains, unlike in most other parts of the country, they can be frequently found in dense woodland such as this. They are a highly territorial and aggressive species and rule over their domain in the same manner of a dictator, driving out any intruders or predators. Although completely unrelated to the great spotted woodpecker and sharing no plumage similarities, their size, shape and structure is surprisingly similar. In fact, they are the only Irish bird likely to be mistaken in flight for a woodpecker since both species have the same bounding flight, like a swell travelling across a calm sea. While I watched the trees overhead, the thrushes often searched for food on the woodland floor around me, only revealing their presence when flying away and giving their long drawn out rattling call. Coincidentally, this sound is remarkably similar to the territorial rattle given by the woodpeckers during the breeding season. At this time of year, when the tree canopy is predominantly bare, it is relatively easy to follow the bird until it lands and to see that it is a mistle thrush. Later in the year, I often see them only briefly in flight through gaps in the foliage, and then it can be impossible to tell whether the bird is a thrush or woodpecker.

By the second week of April, both birds began showing interest in the various existing nest holes in the spanish chestnut tree. There had recently been a small amount of activity at one of the trial holes on the side of the tree. This hole, first excavated last year, had been slightly deepened and enlarged, giving me hope that I would be able to watch the excavation of a nest chamber at close quarters; however, as the days passed without further signs of activity, it became apparent they were merely 'freshening it up' as a way of strengthening their pair bond.

The male was the first to show an interest in a specific nest hole. Early one morning, he landed quite low down on the nesting tree and slowly began hopping upwards. As he passed each of the previous years' nest holes he would pause, and look in, tilting his head sideways as he carefully scrutinised the situation in hand. Was he checking the state of the actual timber itself? Frustratingly, he gave no further indications of what his plans were and flew off in the direction of the garden where the peanut feeders were hanging. The days passed and April drew to a close with neither of the woodpeckers regularly visiting any of the previous years' nest holes. Something was wrong; every year since 2011 there was a nest in the spanish chestnut tree with eggs by the end of April... but not this year.

It was now early May and still there was no sign of eggs being laid. Day after day I watched, but the woodpeckers' activity around the spanish chestnut tree continued to wane. Sometimes hours would pass with no sightings, before the male would quietly arrive and land on his favourite spur and begin to preen. The female was often to be seen landing and peering into the nest hole they used the previous year, almost as though she expected to see something inside. By this stage last year there had been chicks in this very nest hole. I couldn't help but wonder if this was the same female, the mother of Red and Black who had tragically died during their early ventures from this woodland realm...

It was during the second week of May that things took a major change of direction for this pair of woodpeckers. I arrived at the hide in the early evening. The sky was a uniform leaden grey and it had been raining continuously all day. A curtain of rain hung over the glade, and the woodland was echoing to the drumming of raindrops on the canopy against a musical backdrop of water dripping off myriad leaves like distant chimes. After about an hour and a half, as the daylight was making the change towards dusk, one of the pair appeared on the nesting tree, silhouetted against the dull grey sky. It was hard to see any colour, but eventually I spotted the faintest hint of red on the head and knew it was the male. His plumage appeared saturated from the heavy rain, and the feathers on his head were all sticking up strangely, like the hair of a punk rocker. I thought this surprising, as although birds are out in the rain every day they normally don't look like this unless they have just taken a bath. Even then they usually spend a bit of time preening afterwards and get themselves back to a more normal appearance. However, the male made no attempt to preen and, seemingly comfortable with his unkempt appearance, he flew off up the slope and disappeared. I was by now feeling distinctly wet and uncomfortable, and with little likelihood of further sightings that evening, I left the woodland to its nocturnal residents.

The following morning the rain had cleared, and I arrived to find the last vestiges of mist rising from the damp grass as the early sun began drying out the saturated landscape. The soft lime-green leaves of the beech trees had now fully emerged, and the sunlight permeating them bathed the woodland below in a gently flickering viridescence. Over the course of the morning, I heard woodpeckers on several occasions, none of them nearby, yet I never actually saw them.

After a surprisingly disappointing morning, I was making my way back along the track when I saw a woodpecker feeding quietly on a small birch tree. It was the female, and like the male yesterday she also looked saturated, with wet, ruffled feathers and a very punk rocker hairstyle. Before I could get a better look at her she took off and silently flew further into the woodland.

The next day brought another calm, sunny morning and I was in the woodland before 09.00. My arrival was heralded with a loud *KIK* as a woodpecker bounded away from the nesting tree. Quickly, I slipped into the hide and waited for its return. I was still getting myself settled when a loud burst of drumming came from only a couple of metres away: the male was back at the nesting tree and he was not a pretty sight.

He sat on the broken spur jutting out from the side of the tree in full sunshine. Normally the sun would be glinting off his magnificent plumage but now the ebony markings that usually framed his elegantly shaped head and his crimson headpiece were simply gone, as were all the feathers on his head. What fate had befallen him I couldn't begin to guess, but he now looked like a miniature vulture with an almost completely bare head except for a few stubborn, battered feathers near the back of his head, one or two of which were red. Although the rest of his plumage remained largely intact, it was ruffled and dirt-stained with occasional darker streaks suggestive of blood. Unquestionably he had been attacked, but by what and, more importantly, how badly had he been injured? The fact that his injury was at least two days old and that he was actively drumming in front of me suggested that whatever the damage was, it probably was not fatal, at least not for the time being.

He ceased his drumming after a few moments and began preening, before silently flying off. There was no sign of the female that day, and I wondered whether she was incubating somewhere or whether she had been killed during the same incident that befell the male. I was pretty sure I had seen the female the previous day, but now that the male only had one or two visible small red feathers on his head, it would be very hard to tell which bird was which, if the female was equally scalped. The bird I saw the day before, which I took to be the female, had the same spiky unkempt appearance as the male; perhaps it had been the male all along, and I simply hadn't been able to see the few remaining red feathers. Either way, I never saw the female again.

I continued to see the male during my visits, although the sightings were usually brief and uneventful, merely consisting of flight views or brief glimpses of him perching on his favoured branch. However, he seemed to me not just to have lost the lustre of his plumage but also of life, and his presence seemed to fade as he became more and more elusive over the following days...

Eventually, he simply ceased to appear at all, and the woodland felt empty.

9.
ALWAYS ONE STEP AHEAD

BY THE MIDDLE of May I had resigned myself to the fact that there would be no nest in the spanish chestnut tree this year, an event which brought six consecutive years of observations to a close. The injuries seemingly suffered by the male most probably led to his demise, possibly through infection. The fate of the female remained a mystery, but if a predator had indeed attacked the male, it had very possibly gone after the female as well. Despite the sudden cessation of woodpecker sightings, I continued to live in hope that somehow I had misinterpreted the situation, and I continued to visit their territory regularly, although no longer on a daily basis.

It was now approaching June and the surrounding landscape was at its most vibrant with birdsong. The resident blackbirds and song thrushes fought for supremacy with a host of migrant warblers, such as blackcaps and chiffchaffs, for the position of lead singer in the musical ensemble of the woodland canopy singers. However, the absence of the woodpeckers' sharp piercing calls and their far-carrying drumming on the still morning air made this choral event sound insipid to me, incomplete and wanting. If the woodpeckers had survived and had somehow relocated to a different nest site, I figured that by early June I would be able easily to locate the nest by the sound of the young calling. But, despite my endless transects of the woods, there was nothing to indicate the presence of a hitherto undiscovered nest. A ceaseless silence met every effort to listen for the excited begging calls of young woodpeckers eagerly awaiting their parents' return.

With the woodpeckers' unexpected failure to breed and the absence of any nest to study, I now found myself with more time on my hands to explore other habitats in the surrounding area and to discover how the species as a whole was faring. Due to the diligence, perseverance and single-mindedness of a handful of dedicated observers over the years, many great spotted woodpecker nest sites had been dutifully located, recorded and mapped throughout Wicklow.

Because of the species' curious loyalty to nest sites exhibited in Ireland, it was possible for me to visit several nests in a day if I so wished. The Avonmore River cut a twisted track through hundreds of acres of oak woodland, from the glaciated lake of Lough Dan to the Vale of Avoca 20km away, and a surprising number of pairs of great spotted woodpeckers seemed to be attached to this river system. The river itself held no attraction that I knew of to them, and the nests themselves were often located several hundred metres from the river's edge. Nevertheless, by following the course of the river, I knew I would be led through the territories of about twenty pairs of woodpeckers. In addition, there were several other territories, along the various tributaries which flowed into the Avonmore River as it made its long journey to the Wicklow coast.

Although the primary habitat was oakwood, the woodpeckers availed of a range of different breeding habitats, to the extent that no two nest sites were the same, and indeed in many cases their chosen breeding haunts differed enormously. Some nest holes had been occupied for several years, whereas others had been newly-excavated. There were nests high up in the sun-dappled canopy, whilst others had been excavated almost at eye level. Some were stark and obvious in appearance while others were homogenous with their surroundings. To me, all were beautiful, exciting and full of opportunities.

One pair had chosen to nest in the decaying stump of a silver birch on the very edge of an extensive stretch of oakwood. In previous years, they had nested in a small oak, where the nest chamber must have occupied almost the entire width of the actual tree. When I had visited that particular oak earlier in the year, I had seen a pair of great tits carrying small white feathers into the hole with which to line their nest, and I knew then that the woodpeckers had moved on. The birch in which they had chosen to raise this year's family was old and rotten. The base of the trunk was larger than any silver birch I had seen before, and indicated the extreme age of this normally short-lived species. The top of the tree had been snapped off in a storm, so that, instead of the graceful light and delicate canopy so typical of this species, the trunk ended in a jagged scar which marred the beauty of this ethereal tree.

Unexpectedly, the chosen nest tree was not completely surrounded by other trees, but instead was on the boundary of the wood, with open moorland extending from it. In fact, the actual nest hole faced out over the moorland so the youngsters had a most atypical view of the outside world as they stared out across the treeless landscape. By the time this nest had been located, the young were well-developed and were just starting to come up to the entrance to be fed.

It was one of the easiest and most enjoyable woodpecker nests to watch out of all that I had encountered in recent years. The parents were extremely accommodating and did not appear to be bothered at all by my presence, to the extent that no hide or screen was needed; I simply sat out amongst the sun-washed bracken on the open hillside some distance away and watched them through a telescope. Although they were unperturbed by my presence, they were certainly well aware of me sitting in the open nearby, and they would often call several times before arriving back at the nest with food, something that the spanish chestnut pair had never done when I had watched from my hide, well-hidden from their sharp eyes. Aside from calling on their approach, my presence did not seem to affect their behaviour in any way, and after feeding the youngsters, the male would often sit on a short spur alongside the nest hole and preen in the sunshine for minutes on end, totally unfazed. After the disappointing experiences provided to me by my other woodpeckers in the preceding months, and having spent countless hours in a dark hide, it was incredibly refreshing to be able to enjoy the antics of this new family while watching them surrounded by nothing but open hillside. And what antics there were!

As always, it was a challenge to estimate how many chicks were in the nest. I quickly confirmed at least three by the varying amounts of red on their crowns. They were a boisterous family, full of noise and action. Once a few days had passed and they had grown strong enough to cling to the entrance hole, they would constantly scrabble and squabble as each jostled for position in an attempt to reach the food before its siblings.

The nest hole was situated roughly 10m above the ground, just below a jagged stump where the top of the tree had broken off. The hole itself had been excavated where a bough had been ripped off and the sapwood exposed. I figured that the centre of the tree must have been well-rotted, as the nest chamber extended to the outer bark and was actually visible to me watching from the hillside. I had never come across this at any previous nest, and it made for fascinating viewing; the cracks and clefts in the birch bark enabled me to spot slivers of activity as the birds jockeyed for position inside the nesting cavity. Sometimes a hint of plumage would be visible; a glimpse of pied feathering and even an occasional flash of cerise.

One morning, while I was watching a chick constantly calling to be fed, a movement on the bark below the nest caught my attention. What appeared to be a small thin snake was winding its way amongst the ivy leaves which encircled the tree: one of the young woodpeckers inside the tree was discovering the outside world using his tongue. Parts of the outer bark of the tree were crumbling, and as the young woodpecker probed with his tongue from the inside, these started to collapse and fall away. A gentle shower of bark fragments and pieces of grey-green lichen descended to the ground below as I watched. The youngster carried on exploring what was beyond the wooden walls of its home and kept the tip of its bill pressed against the crack in the bark, its tongue flickering in and out, extending several centimetres each time, along the crevices on the outside of the tree. All the time this was happening, one sibling kept up a continuous *Keek... Keek... Keek* from the entrance hole, while another was just visible behind him, scrabbling to oust him from the prime position. I was unable to see whether the young woodpecker was actually trying to feed or was simply exploring what lay beyond the confines of the nesting chamber. Strangely, his endeavours reminded me of a chick hatching from an egg; something I've seen many times in the past with other species of bird. In both cases, the chicks were breaking out from the confines of one world into the vast expanse of a new one, but in the case of the woodpeckers they had to break out twice, once from the egg and again from the nest cavity.

The fact that the walls of the nesting chamber were literally crumbling at the touch left me in no doubt that this nest would not be used next season; it simply wouldn't be there any longer. More worryingly was the possibility that the youngsters would be exposed to predators before being mature enough to fly. Pine martens were certainly a potential risk, because it was now late in the season and any female pine marten would have a family of hungry kits in tow. The noise from this particular family of woodpeckers was a lot louder than most of the others I had observed, making them easier to locate. As I arrived in the woods I could hear the chicks calling from several hundred metres away, and I imagined that a sharp-eared pine marten would hear them from twice that distance. If so, the crumbling walls of the nest chamber would offer no protection whatsoever. Although pine martens will climb trees, they are not arboreal in the same manner as a red squirrel, and I was hopeful since the nest was so high up, compared to other woodpecker nests nearby, that it might appear less attractive to a pine marten.

As with the woodpeckers that had nested in the spanish chestnut tree, there was also a peanut feeder in the vicinity of this nest. Although, as far as I could tell from my observations, only the male ever availed of this food source. It was located on the far side of the open hillside at an isolated farmhouse which lay about a kilometre away. Given the amount of open land between the nest and the feeder, I often wondered how he had ever found the garden in the first place, especially given that it wasn't even visible from any aspect of the woodland. After feeding the youngsters, he would typically perch on the nearby spur for a quick preen before bounding high across the open moor and being lost to view over the hillside horizon. It would usually be about fifteen minutes before he returned with a bill full of peanut fragments. The length of time he took to complete this journey suggested that he may have been feeding himself as much as gathering food for the family. Unlike the female, who seemed to confine her efforts to seeking food in the surrounding canopy, the male was much more innovative in his approach to foraging.

As well as locating the peanuts, he found another food source amongst the actual bracken where I sat. The unfurling bracken fronds, shaped like bishops' croziers, still formed an incomplete canopy, and the forest of slender green stems rose out of a dense, bronze mulch of dead fronds. It was into this miniature woodland that the male woodpecker kept disappearing on his foraging excursions. Sometimes he seemed quite oblivious to my presence and landed only 15m from me, completely lost from view in the contrasting green and brown landscape. His progress was marked by the movement of the tall bracken fronds and by the continuous *Kik* calls he made as he sought his quarry. Occasionally he would hop into a small clearing in the bracken and tilt his head sideways to try to get a better look at the ground.

On the ground, woodpeckers present a most bizarre sight; the distinctive triangular shape, created by their wide shoulders and straight-backed posture as they lean away from the trunk onto their tail feathers, is designed for a life on the side of a tree; on the ground it simply makes them look pot-bellied and ungainly. It was quite surprising to hear the male calling so frequently while foraging in cover which could easily have been concealing a predator such as a fox or stoat, either of which would quickly have dispatched him. Also, it occurred to me that the food source must have been particularly profitable to lure him from the relative safety of his more usual tree dwelling habits.

I never managed to identify this food source, but I suspect that he most likely had been collecting ants. To my cost, I knew from sitting amongst the bracken myself that there were large colonies of ants within it and on several occasions I was forced to move as I had inadvertently sat on an ants' nest. Other species of woodpecker, such as the green woodpecker, which is not found in Ireland but does occur in Great Britain and across much of Europe, regularly feed on ants. However, aside from this male, I have never seen a great spotted woodpecker foraging in this manner. As with the other nests I watched at this time of year, both parents started feeding their hungry offspring, usually beginning at around 05.00 and carrying on without stopping until well after 21.00, with visits taking place every ten minutes or thereabouts throughout the day. The youngsters successfully left the nest over a period of two days, with the first departing shortly after sunrise and its siblings following in their own time. My final visit was greeted by the inevitable silence that signalled both success and the end of my moorland sojourn.

Most of the great spotted woodpeckers in County Wicklow had chosen to nest in the mixed oak habitat that occurs along most of the valleys, both glaciated and riverine, which cut through the Wicklow Mountains. Native woods with a high proportion of deciduous trees offer far richer biodiversity than those with a high proportion of conifers, and the lack of large tracts of these trees has long been cited as a reason for woodpeckers not previously having bred in Ireland. It was a surprise, therefore, to encounter another pair which, rather than seeking out deciduous trees, had opted to actively avoid them.

The Scots Pine plantation in which the woodpecker pair in question lived was located on the top of a hill, far above the sheltered valley floor, and it covered an area of about 1km². It was a mature commercial plantation that had been planted over eighty years previously, and part of it had already been harvested and replanted with a new crop of fast-growing spruce trees. It was a perfect example of the monoculture, which typifies modern forestry plantations, and the mature trees stood, evenly spaced like ranks of soldiers, as far as the eye could see.

The silence of a coniferous forest when compared to the living vibrancy of the nearby oakwoods is startling. Whereas the latter were filled with the chorus of warblers, thrushes and other songbirds, this forest echoed to the sound of the wind through the towering trees above, interspersed with the high-pitched calls of goldcrests and coal tits, the only two species of birds which seem at home in these dark, dank habitats. As the trees in a forestry plantation are fast-growing and are typically harvested before they begin to show much sign of decay, there are usually very few trees that provide deadwood for woodpeckers to feed on. Yet despite this, one pair of great spotted woodpeckers had made this foreboding place their home for at least the preceding four years, and possibly even for some years prior to that. A decaying tree stump, one of a mere handful in this forest, had provided their home, and several nest holes had been created over the years, one directly above the other, with the result that a 'totem pole' effect had been created. Sadly, this visually appealing natural feature did not remain, and one winter the rotting stump collapsed, forcing the birds to relocate to a new tree stump located 200m distant. Within a relatively short period of time they had recreated the totem pole effect, so that the new nesting tree also sported several holes both directly and indirectly above the original nest hole.

In previous years, this pair of woodpeckers had been among the last of those being observed to lay eggs. Whether this was related in any way to their chosen territory being located in a coniferous wood is hard to say but the overall lower biodiversity of this type of habitat certainly could not have helped. This year the chicks had hatched around the first week of June and were due to leave the nest in late June or early July. However, shortly before they were fully mature, the nest fell unexpectedly quiet. An examination of the tree showed that a large ragged hole had been hacked into the back of the tree, just below the entrance hole; unquestionably the work of a pine marten. Being so late in the season and with the chicks at their most vocal, this had coincided with the time of year when a pine marten family was on the move and at its' most voracious with so many mouths to feed. The rotting pine stump had offered no resistance to the sharp-clawed predator, which probably took only minutes to break through the walls of the nesting chamber before simply dropping the helpless chicks one at a time to the waiting mouths below. Less than a decade previously, neither of these two species had been present in this wood, yet now they were locked in a struggle to find equilibrium. Only future decades will reveal the outcome on the distribution of both these range-expanding species.

Shortly after the demise of these youngsters, I received an unexpected call from the owners of the garden where Red and Black had both perished the previous year. Despite the fact that no pair had bred this year in the spanish chestnut tree, two youngsters had nevertheless arrived in the garden and were now feeding from the peanut feeder. It was by now late in the season, several weeks after young birds would usually arrive at these garden feeders, and because no adults were accompanying them, I felt in all likelihood that they were from a more distant territory and were simply roaming around the district in search of food. The youngsters carried on visiting the garden for several days before a startling revelation emerged.

They were now being accompanied by a third bird with a completely bald head!

I arrived at the garden early the next morning. Despite being early in the day, there was already heat in the air, for it was now high summer and the tracks through the copse alongside me were vibrating to the endless humming of thousands of insect wings in the still air. Above me the pale denim blue sky, forsaken of cloud, told of yet another day under the blazing sun, and not even a breath of wind stirred the nearby copse of birch trees. I didn't have long to wait before a series of *Kik... Kik... Kik* calls sounded from them, followed by movement amongst the canopy. First one, then both youngsters emerged from cover and began flying down to the feeder, scattering the blue tits, robins and dunnocks and causing them to dive into the cover of nearby bushes. Unlike Red and Black the previous year, both of these youngsters had very similar crimson-coloured crowns which extended from their foreheads to the back of their heads. Interestingly, one of them was darkly stained on his front, almost like he had landed in oil or some other dark and sticky substance. Young woodpeckers do not return to the nest to roost at night, but rather roost on a sheltered bough. It occurred to me that perhaps this youngster had been roosting against one of the large cedars in the nearby estates and had become covered in the resin which often coats the bark at this time of year. Suddenly, a loud *KIK* sounded from behind me, and a third woodpecker moved into view. This one had a bald head.

It was almost two months since I had seen him, and he was still as bald as a vulture, while the few remaining red feathers at the back of his head were still clinging stubbornly to his wrinkled parchment-like skin. Other than that, he seemed to be in good health, and whatever near-tragedy had befallen him the previous spring obviously had not fatally injured him, as I had led myself to believe. Naturally, I was relieved to see that he was alive but I also felt frustrated – or, to be honest, hoodwinked. After all my efforts and endeavours, not alone had my spanish chestnut pair survived when I had convinced myself they were dead, but they had even managed to rear two youngsters completely unbeknownst to me, despite my having searched the glade and surrounding area so many times listening for youngsters calling. Where had I gone wrong?

Looking over my notes during the following weeks, a possible scenario came to light. Traditionally, these two woodpeckers had brought their youngsters to the peanut feeder garden about a week after they had fledged. Assuming this had been the case this time around then the youngsters had to have fledged extremely late; later, indeed, than in any previous year, and possibly latest amongst all of that year's breeding pairs, despite the fact that in previous years they had been the earliest to fledge.

Everything had seemed to be on course until late April, when we know that a predator must have injured the male, and possibly the female too. I suspect that they were attacked at the nesting tree prior to egg laying and then decided to abandon that tree, quite reasonably believing that it was no longer safe. They must then have decided either to excavate a new nest hole nearby or to use a nearby pre-existing roosting hole. This relocation of premises would have set them back about four weeks, so by the time I was searching for calling youngsters in the woodland they may not yet have hatched, leading me to the wrong conclusion that they were not even there. I also wondered whether their narrow escape may also have made them more secretive, and therefore less likely to call as they foraged in the trees.

But what was the incident that had caused all this? What predator could scalp a woodpecker, but not kill it? Interestingly, later that summer an event was recounted to me that may reveal the answer. Another observer filming woodpeckers at the nest captured the incredible sight of a sparrowhawk landing at the nest hole, and reaching into it with its foot and grabbing a young woodpecker by the head with its talons. It was unsuccessful in getting the bird out from the nest, but it did take a few feathers with it as it flew off. This astonishing observation revealed the sheer adaptability of supreme predators such as sparrowhawks and the seemingly never-ending struggle of the great spotted woodpecker to survive. The good news is that the chicks in that particular nest successfully fledged a few days later.

So perhaps that was the missing piece of the puzzle. Had the male been roosting in the nest hole, dozing with his eyes half-closed, when the small circle of light above him was suddenly blocked by the arrival of a sparrowhawk? Had he frantically flapped around as the needle-sharp claws searched around inside the trunk before grasping him by the head and trying to pull him out? If indeed this is what happened, and the male somehow escaped minus a few feathers, it is quite likely he and his mate would have abandoned that nest cavity and even the whole tree, and would then have excavated another nest in a more secure location. The female may have escaped the attack, but the trauma experienced at the nest site would quite likely also have discouraged her from remaining.

Of course, this is all pure speculation on my part and as I watched the youngsters on the peanut feeder in the company of their father, I knew that I would never know the full story of what had happened in the woods this year. Woodpeckers, like most birds, are often one step ahead of us, while we simply run behind trying to catch up and then attempt to put the pieces of the story together. After the previous season's tragic ending, I was simply happy that the pair had survived and had managed to get two youngsters off to a good start in life. I didn't yet know the answers to a great many questions about their lives and about the woodland realm in which they lived in but I was certain of one thing... the story was not over.

February 2017 was wet; it had been a mild winter in the Wicklow Mountains, and the little snow that fell remained stubbornly only on the high tops. Deluges of rainfall however poured across the landscape as Storm 'Doris' ripped through the countryside, followed only days later by Storm 'Ewan', with numerous nameless weather systems following shortly thereafter. The rivers, engorged and swollen by the endless runoff from the saturated hillsides, rose and burst their banks. Stag-headed oaks, no longer able to resist the relentless power of the wind, while trying to maintain a foothold in the sodden soil, lay across the landscape like fallen giants... but the spanish chestnut tree remained steadfast.

I stood before it one morning in late March, as the rain fell softly and a woodpecker called distantly. I was watching a blue tit struggling with a feather almost as big as itself, trying to carry it to where it was making its nest in a nearby tree. As I watched its Herculean effort, I noticed a blaze of red on the tree behind it. Adjusting my binoculars, the image of a female great spotted woodpecker came into view. She was engrossed in pecking at some grey lichens on the branch upon which she was perched, and she seemed utterly unaware of my presence, or unbothered by it at any rate. It had been several months since I had seen a female woodpecker here, and as I watched her I noticed that her underparts were not the usual pristine white but were suffused in pink, and also that the blaze of red under her tail was not actually as deep in tone as I had previously thought. This, then had to be a different bird, and judging by her muted colouring, she was very possibly a young bird from last year. Before I could see any more details, she took off and silently flew further into the depths of the woods and out of sight, leaving me with yet more unanswered questions.

As I stood there in the glade looking in the direction in which she had flown, the male woodpecker commenced drumming several hundred metres away in the opposite direction. I smiled, and after placing my rucksack, containing my flask and biscuits, into the hide, I bounded down the slope in the direction in which the female had just flown…

A new season had begun.

AFTERWORD

IT WAS LATE IN the evening, shortly before sunset, and I was lying on the garden trampoline staring at a slowly deepening blue sky as the sun began to drop towards the horizon. The setting sun was emblazoning the sky with a pinkish-red hue, streaked with amber, dotted with small white cumulus clouds which had a surprising habit of springing into existence out of nothing, like slowly exploding popcorn. A male great spotted woodpecker had a daily routine of flying over the garden towards the woodland, which contained the spanish chestnut tree, 2km distant. However, aside from a few swallows and house martins, nothing was to be seen. I was still staring at the sky when my six-year-old son arrived 'What are you doing Daddy?' 'Watching clouds', I replied, lost in my thoughts. He climbed up beside me. 'I'll watch too', he said. I showed him the clouds forming out of the nothingness and slowly expanding into trails, wisps and whorls like balls of cotton.

'Are they being born?', he asked. This seemed a far simpler and more beautiful explanation than trying to explain that they formed when rising warm air cools to the point where water vapour molecules condense to form droplets or ice crystals and become visible as clouds. 'Yes', I said 'I suppose they are', and we both sat quietly watching clouds being born. Not surprisingly, my three-year-old daughter then arrived, having been walking around looking for 'the boys'. We told her we were watching clouds being born, so up she came and lay down alongside us. 'I see one', she piped 'I see a new-born baby cloud'. The three of us lay there as the painted sky turned towards darkening amethyst, watching new-born baby clouds materializing in front of us.

As if on cue, a bullet-shaped arrow bounded overhead. *Kik* it called, before disappearing into the smoky blue distance. Was it going to the spanish chestnut tree, I wondered? Did it matter?

To see the landscape through the eyes of a child is to enter a realm of magical light and beauty, filled with wondrous sights and experiences. Yet it is a land denied to so many, stifled by the staleness and stagnation that modern day life inflicts upon them. Social media, the internet and Google now dominate and close our minds, seemingly providing the knowledge we crave in an instant. But, for me, knowledge without experience is worthless, nothing but the regurgitation of the life experiences of others. While some of the observations I made could probably have been found through an internet search, no aspect of technology or measurement of science could reproduce those experiences – the sharpness of the air on those still winter mornings, the scent of soil beginning to warm in the lengthening light of the spring sun, the weight of a speckled wood butterfly alighting on my bare arm or the shafts of sunlight turning the amber leaves to tangerine as they slip through the autumn tree canopy.

In writing this book, I have sought to convey the images that accompanied me throughout my woodland ventures. I hope I have brought the magic and wonder of that realm to you, the reader, and that you have shared with me the sights, sounds and magic of what nature has to offer. That hidden landscape, still so vibrant and fresh in my mind, is there for all to experience, and I encourage you to experience that wonderful world for yourself.

BIRDWATCH IRELAND
Fostering Children's Imaginations

CHILDREN ARE BORN with an innate, natural curiosity about the world around them; they love to see the moon, to watch birds, to reach out and touch animals and to pick flowers. Sadly, and all too soon, this fascination with life has to compete for its very existence as the so-called 'pressures of the modern age' vie for supremacy. We now live in an electronic age; this is not necessarily a bad thing, but sadly many children, often from as young as the age of three, now have more exposure to YouTube, web browsers and online gaming than the natural world they are part of.

Usually the responsibility of encouraging children and developing their interest in the world around them falls on the shoulders of parents or older relations. When I was a young teenager, my parents paid my membership fee for BirdWatch Ireland, since I lacked the means to do so myself. Likewise, they paid for the countless wildlife magazines I wanted but hadn't the money to buy. There was no way of knowing whether I would 'grow out' of this interest or maintain it – it was a chance they had to take. By enrolling me as a member of BirdWatch Ireland, they gave me an outlet for my interest, which led to real friendships that have lasted a lifetime; something unlikely to happen by fostering a child's interest in YouTube!

But, like any worthwhile investment, to truly foster a child's imagination and their interest in birds takes time, so don't just enrol them as members for one year: do it for several years, until such time as they can afford to pay for it themselves. Or why not enrol the whole family by taking out a family membership, and make BirdWatch Ireland part of 'family day out' trips?

Contact BirdWatch Ireland for details at 01-2819878 or www.birdwatchireland.ie.